In Other Words

j. r. Barnes

Published by j. r. barnes, 2024.

IN OTHER WORDS

First edition. October 17, 2024.

ISBN: 979-8227394705

Written by j. r. Barnes.

Also by j. r. Barnes

Sailing Home
The Blue Rose
In Other Words

To my daughter - Michelle Kerns

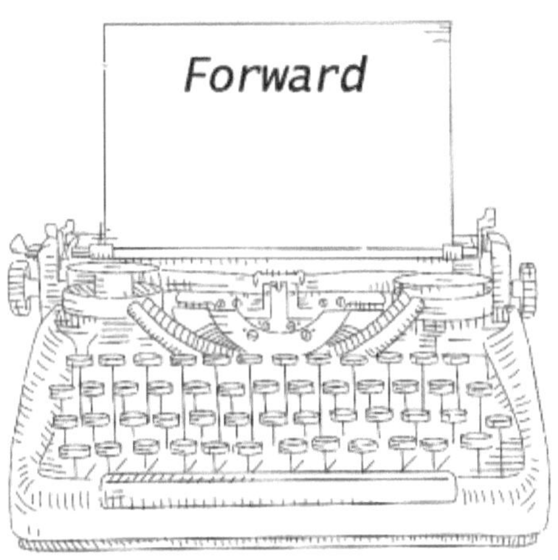

The word essay literally means an attempt or effort. I only recently discovered this little gem. I had always believed essays to be formal dissertations on a given subject by persons well informed and academically credentialed.

As best as I can recall, I was in the sixth grade the first time I was asked to write an essay, and I thought the teacher was expecting w-a-y too much of me. What the hell did I know about anything? I developed a dread of writing essays even though I had, unbeknownst to me, been writing essays all along.

As far back as I can remember, I started writing down my thoughts on everything that crossed my mind. I had written a little blurb titled "I Talk To The Trees." My mother discovered it and asked me if I actually talked to trees. I told her, "Yes, I do." She appeared to be a little alarmed and asked if they also talked to me. "Not in words like you and I use," I answered. "So, in other words, they don't actually speak to you, right?" she asked. "Well, yes, they do—in other words." She let the subject drop.

Words are such clumsy things. We struggle to find the right ones to express our amorphous feelings and condense the mist of our ideas into an understandable form. We use them as an attempt, an effort to communicate who we are, how we are, and why we are who we are; where we are coming from, where we are now, and where we are going; our ideas, our doubts, and our beliefs. We use metaphors, analogies, and parables to help paint a picture that, while not always an accurate portrayal, strives to illustrate a deeper reality. A flat surface may become a hill to convey the struggle inherent in a person's journey. A character from one story might just visit another tale because they are needed to help the story come into full bloom—but always we fall short because words are not the object, the feeling, or the idea—words are only symbols of these things. Still, we do the best we can.

I offer to you in these pages my best attempt, my best effort, to express who it is that I am—in other words.

IN OTHER WORDS

CONTENTS

Holding on / Letting Go

On My Way To Becoming Rick

11/04/2008

Musings

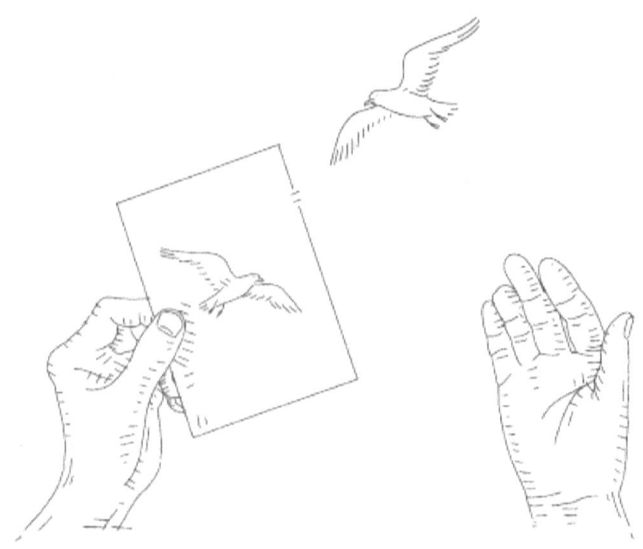

Holding On / Letting Go

Sally's Gravity

We were only a few pages into the beginning of a story that had yet to develop much of a plot, and much of the narrative was but a loose-knit gathering of flashing firefly memories, but this I remember.

We, five first graders, would gather in a cluster at the foot of Douglas Street Hill and begin our daily trek up the steep slope on our way to Miss Delaney's first grade class at Mount Ivy Elementary School. To say we *walked* up Douglas Street Hill would only belie our efforts—we climbed. Our formation was the same each day: Roy and Worley in front, Freddie and I at the rear, and Sally tucked in between the four of us.

Sally was a frail (we would have said 'boney), small cage of a black girl from, literally and figuratively, the other side of the tracks, and by the time she met up with us at the foot of the hill, she would have already walked a small child's mile, but here she came, riding on those two skinny legs, her head tilted back and her eyes scanning the rise that lay before her, as if the distance alone were not burden enough. Upon her arrival, we would assemble into formation and proceed up the quarter-mile incline.

On our very first ascent, about halfway up, our steps had become too small and too tiresome to justify the effort it took to continue on.

Between deep breaths, one of us managed to say, "Let's stop here, (pant)...so Sally, (pant)...can catch her breath."

'Here', was Ole Mister Woodfork's place, an old ramshackle of a house that was gradually, if stubbornly, losing its battle with the gravity of Douglas Street Hill.

Mister Woodfork was a time-worn and caution-cured elderly black gentleman, with big round, off-white, and baby blue eyes protruding out of their sockets as if he had long been searching for something. His skin hung loose on his bones, and the veins in his hands pushed the thin black skin up to reveal their staggered path, resembling a 3D map of several rivers merging and parting across rough terrain.

We would find him sitting out on his porch in his cane rocking chair every morning, come wind, rain, sleet, heat, or cold winter's snow. Stingy with his words, he just sat there, looking out across Douglas Street, staring at something only he could see. For our part, we didn't know what to say to him, and I doubt he had much to say to us.

He gathered us into his eyes and said, "You chilluns, sit yourself down here on the porch and rest a while."

Mister Woodfork's porch was a worn-down wooden structure sitting high off the sidewalk on the downhill side and level with the sidewalk on the uphill side. It became our regular roadside rest on school days, and he began putting out cold water in paper cups on hot days and hot cocoa in Styrofoam cups on cold days. Every so often, he placed a giant open container of horehound candy on the porch. We'd load our pockets full, thank Ol' Mister Woodfork, and head on up Douglas Street Hill sucking on horehound candy like a big block Ford motor with a brand new carburetor. Ol' Mister Woodfork would almost break a smile and give a slight nod in the affirmative as he watched us chug on up the hill.

One chilly March morning, Sally didn't show up, and the walk up Douglas Street felt a little clumsier for her absence. When we reached Ol' Mister Woodfork's porch, he didn't say a word. He scanned us briefly in search of Sally and then resumed his stare, looking out across Douglas Street. We drank our hot cocoa in silence and then continued our march up Douglas Street Hill to school.

About a week later, on a blustery March morning, Sally stood waiting for us at the bottom of the hill. She wavered a bit within the small space she occupied between us, and during our climb that morning, she twice stumbled and almost fell before Freddie and I braced her up between us.

When we reached Ol' Mister Woodfork's place, Sally was struggling to catch her breath. He kept an eye on her the whole time we rested there drinking our hot cocoa, and as we prepared to leave, he said,

"You young'uns, get along to your learnin' now. Sally won't be goin' no further with ya today."

With that, we all waved goodbye to Sally and hiked up to school. I think each of us wondered what was wrong with Sally, but no one wanted to be the one to bring it up.

In the days that followed, Sally's absence took on a heavier tone. It wasn't her conversation we missed; she hardly ever said a word. Maybe it was something as simple as the hollowness of her missing footsteps, or the change in the constellation of bodies for lack of a certain center of gravity, or something much more profound.

On a warm Thursday morning, the day before Good Friday, when we stopped by Ol' Mister Woodfork's place, he was sitting upright in his cane rocking chair, dressed in an old black crumpled suit and tie that matched the somber, worn, and tired look on his face. The table at his side was bare of refreshments, except for four small bags of Easter jellybeans. We sat there and stared at him as he gazed out across Douglas Street, tears welling up in his eyes.

He handed each of us a bag of jellybeans and said, "You chilluns, run along to yur lessons now."

As we stood up to leave, Ol' Mister Woodfork eased himself off the porch and started walking down Douglas Street Hill.

My past has taken on enough mass to exert a kind of historical gravity, and my memories of childhood are many, most of them happy. But some memories anchor us more than others, and I am drawn forever back to the memory of that blustery March morning in 1956, when we walked up Douglas Street Hill with our friend Sally for the last time.

The Last Word On Uncle Chaucer

Uncle Chaucer was dead.

I was seven years old and had no idea what 'dead' meant. But, as it turns out, neither did anyone else. The difference was that I knew I didn't know, so there was no point in pretending otherwise.

I wasn't exactly close to my great-uncle Chaucer. I had only seen him two or three times in my seven years, which, as I was to learn later, was about all most people could handle in one lifetime.

"A little Chance goes a long way," my relatives used to say. Everyone called him Chance.

He lived alone in a two-room apartment—no telephone, no television, never owed a car. I never saw my great-uncle Chance outside of his apartment; for all I know, he may have spent his entire life inside that little twin cubicle. If you wanted to see Chance, you had to go to him; he was not about to come to you.

He was, apparently, happy with this arrangement, and so, I gathered, were his relatives—all except for my father. My father seemed to be fond of him, and Chance seemed to return the sentiment. He always surrendered a brief smile when my father came to visit, but his lips flattened back into a straight-thin line at the sight of my brother and me. Save for a simple recognition of our presence, we may as well have stayed in the car. He made no attempt to entertain us. I don't know if he lacked the desire, the know-how, or both, but when you're seven years old and being ignored by someone ten times your age, it doesn't really matter.

During these visits, there was literally nothing for my brother and me to do but sit quietly on an old, overstuffed green sofa and fidget while the two men sat at a small, well-worn wood plank table, chatting and sharing crackers, cheese, and summer sausage washed down with glass after glass of German beer.

The conversations always started off with both of them complaining about how idiotic most people are. At first, they seemed to be angry about having to occupy the same planet with a sub-species of boobs. But as their supply of beer dwindled, their mood toward their fellow sapiens turned to one of amusement. I remember following their conversation up to this point on a couple of occasions, beyond which they would laugh out loud and speak in incomplete sentences while I sat there smiling ear to ear in reaction to their laughter without so much as a farthing of an idea of what was so funny.

Great-Uncle Chaucer died on August 1st, 1956. It was a matter-of-fact kind of death. No one seemed surprised. No one reacted in any way that can be associated with remorse. Chaucer was dead. That was that.

My father took care of the funeral arrangements and asked me to attend. My great-aunt Mel, Chaucer's sister, watched over me while dad was busy with funeral things. She was the default family historian and had filled our ears with stories about various members of our father's family. But in my seven years, I had never heard her so much as mention Chaucer's name. Why the omission? In the telling of all of her stories, she never spoke ill of anyone. Never! I could only surmise from all of this that there simply wasn't anything good to say about my great-uncle Chance.

The funeral was very brief, with lots of talk about Jesus, God's wrath, and the torments of Hell. I suppose they were alluding to Chaucer's present address and urging us to bid him "adieu" one last time, the righteous among us, to never see his face again.

Afterward, as people filed by the casket, Aunt Mel held my hand as we stood in line, and I could hear the remarks of the various passersby as they stopped to give their final respects.

"He's better off now," one remarked.

"I doubt it," replied someone else.

"Nastiest S.O.B. I ever knew," said another.

"Now's not the time for that, Harold," came the reprimand.

"He's proof that only the good die young," said a man, laughing at his own quip.

"Such a wasted life," the woman in front of us said.

Aunt Mel paused before the casket and stared down at Chaucer for a moment, tears glistening her eyes.

"That Chaucer," she said in a soft reverent voice, "he sure could whistle."

Magellan and the Desire for Justice

Madge. When people referred to him at all, they referred to him in a scoffing tone, as "Madge." I remember wondering why, but I wasn't about to ask. I figured it was some sort of inside joke I wouldn't understand anyway, so why bother? Sometimes it's best that way.

I first met Madge when I was about thirteen years old. The back wheel of my three-speed bicycle had disintegrated, and I was sitting on the curb in front of his house, pretending to myself that I was figuring it out and that my two bare hands and I could somehow fix it. Madge walked up, stood over me, and said, "Bring it into my garage, and we'll see what we can salvage."

I had seen Madge before, working in his front yard or driving his 1951 Sky Blue Studebaker. I had noticed that he was always alone, but I hadn't really given it much thought. Adults were of a vast variety, most of which I didn't understand.

We were only a couple of steps into the immaculately clean interior of his—was this really a garage?—when I slowed to a halt to scan the wonder that surrounded me. Tools galore, hung with care, adorned all four walls. Machines, large and small, chrome and red and yellow and black, mounted on tables; neatly piled stacks of metal and wood; drawer after drawer of nuts and bolts and screws and nails and washers; and odd-shaped things I had never seen before. It was the most marvelous collection of God-Knows-What I had ever encountered.

He had a special tool for taking the tire off of the rim, another for removing spokes, and yet another for revealing the inner workings of things without resorting to a hammer or a saw.

In no time, he had the hub of my drive wheel laid out in pieces in front of him.

"Ah-hah!" he exclaimed. "Here is the problem. You'll never be able to buy just this one part. They want to sell you the whole hub. Well, for their greed, they'll get nothing."

And with that said, he went to a box filled with pieces of metal. He pulled craggy scrap out of the box and began cutting it, bending it, shaping it, and drilling it until it fit perfectly inside the hub of the back wheel. He reassembled the entire rim, hub, spokes and all, filled the re-mounted tire with air, and sent me wheeling away.

The following day, I wanted to do something to thank him. Money, of course, was out of the question. I pedaled my easy-riding bicycle over to his house and knocked on his door.

"Yes?" he said, answering the door as if I were selling something.

"Thank you for fixing my bicycle. I would like to repay you, but I ain't got no money," I said. "Maybe I could—"

"That isn't necessary," he interrupted, and he closed the door.

I disagreed.

One summer day, after confirming he wasn't home, I took my father's lawn mower over to Madge's house and began mowing the lawn. Because I am lazy, mowing the lawn really meant, mowing *most* of the lawn. Those troublesome spots in-between, around, and under things don't really count as 'mowing the lawn.' That is called landscaping, and I am definitely *not* a landscaper.

Lazy people like to daydream, especially when confronted with a repetitive task such as mowing a lawn. I can only make such work tolerable by pretending I am doing something else, and so, I transform my lawnmower into many interesting things, like a bulldozer, a gargantuan combine, or a military deforestation tool—the list goes on and on.

I was in the middle of one such daydream when I heard a voice coming from the wide-awake world.

"No, no, no... That is not how you mow a lawn."

But for inflection, it could have been my father. I turned to find Madge staring with disapproval at his once well-coiffed lawn.

"Here, let me show you," he said, and he took the lawn mower from my hands and gave me a thorough lesson in the art of mowing a lawn. When he had finished, his lawn was the 'cover of a magazine', perfect.

"That is how you mow a lawn," he informed me.

"Well, I was doing my best," I countered. "It's the thought that counts."

"No, no, it is not," he replied. "It is the results that count. And as far as thought goes, you put no more thought into this than a chimpanzee would have. Now come inside for some of the best lemonade you have ever had in your young life."

Thirst outweighing insult I accepted his invitation.

As the summer progressed, so did our friendship, and he insisted I call him by his real name, Magellan.

"Although," he added, "no one has called me Magellan since my mother and father both passed away many years ago. God rest their souls."

He would often call out to me as I rode by his house on my fully functioning bicycle.

"Hey, if you have a moment, I have something that just may interest you," and he would show me some new gadget or thing-a-ma-bob he had come up with. Other times he would invite me in for lemonade and ask me what I thought about this or that theory of his.

For example, he thought there should be 13 months in a year, each containing 28 days, or exactly 4 weeks. That would leave one day a year (two on leap year) without a monthly home. On that day (he chose what is now July 2nd, the halfway point of the year), we each get to celebrate anything we please—he was very serious about this.

Sometimes he would invite me along on one of his long walks around town and tell me about the history of a particular building or how this street came to be named 'Carmine Avenue', and he loved to talk at length about the decline of architecture and civility.

One day we paused in front of the Justice Building downtown, and he said, "This is where people come for justice," he explained, "but it actually resides here," and he held his open hand upon my heart. "Justice first requires a desire for justice. There is so much work to be done."

As our friendship matured, I couldn't help but wonder, 'Am I his only friend?' If so, his lack of friends didn't seem to bother him a great deal. He never spoke to me of loneliness or depression, except to once say, "I don't know where some people find the time to be so miserable."

Sometimes late at night, things would occur to me, and I could hardly wait until the following morning to stop by Magellan's on my way to school and discuss them with him.

One such morning, as I rode up to Magellan's house, I noticed several policemen surrounding the premise. I asked an officer what was going on and was told to 'go on about my business.'

Later the next day, a woman who lived down the street explained to me that someone she referred to as a homophobe had beaten Magellan to death with a baseball bat. It wasn't a robbery; nothing was stolen—except his life.

There were only a handful of people at Magellan's funeral—not that he would have minded. Knowing nothing about his family or background, I wondered who these all too few people were. After they left, I never saw them again. Over the course of the next few months, his house was sold and all of his possessions were auctioned off. By December, it was as if he had never existed.

The person responsible for his death was never caught, and for the longest time after his death, I would look at random people and wonder if they were the homophobe who murdered my friend. I remember thinking I was being unfair by staring at people and having these thoughts about them, but what is a boy to do when his friend is ripped from his life by such a hateful act?

Sometimes there is no justice save that which resides in the heart of a single person. Magellan existed, goddamn it! He existed, and he was my friend. I decided to make one day a year, July 2nd, Magellan's Day. I celebrate it by doing all or most of the things that I have put off doing, and I talk to myself all day as if Magellan were here, because, in a very real way, he is. I will do my best to speak out for Magellan as long as I exist. For reasons related to justice, it is important for me to do that. "Justice first requires a desire for justice," he told me.

And so it is that Magellan and I ask of you, dear reader, "Desire justice."

Mister Masters' Last Concert

I began my musical education in earnest in the sixth grade. I spent most of that year learning how to make a sound resembling music through the coiled tube of my cornet. After a year of practicing half an hour a day, seven days a week, I could play a few songs I had no desire to play; "Red River Valley" and 'She'll Be Comin' Around the Mountain" stand out prominently. I had also learned a few of the basic musical scales, but I wasn't sure why I had bothered to learn them.

Entering the seventh grade meant I could try out for the Junior High Concert Band. My repertoire being as meager as it was, I remember wondering if I should even bother. They probably wouldn't be playing She'll Be Comin' Around The Mountain, and I hadn't received a single request for the chromatic scale. Had I been trying out for the concert band simply because my parents wanted me to, I may not have been quite so nervous, but this was something I wanted to do. I had always wanted to be a musician, even if 'always' isn't a particularly muscular word when you are only eleven years old.

The bandmaster was an older gentleman named Mister Masters, a name conjuring up images of Beethoven, Wagner, and other musical giants. Through the eyes of a thirteen-year-old cornet player, Mister Masters stood at a height that can only be described as stature. He filled out a suit of clothing without appearing overweight or particularly muscular, and yet he had a muscular demeanor about him. Powerful is perhaps a better word. His long, untamed gray hair only added to the mystique, and when he looked at you with those intense blue eyes, it was impossible to look away—you were in his grasp.

As I sat out in the corridor waiting for my turn to audition, another contestant named Larry Throckmorton (whom I had never seen before and never saw again) felt it was his duty to warn me of Mister Masters' very strict and demanding nature. "He simply does not tolerate mistakes," he said. For some stupid reason, I thanked him for telling me this. I knew that Mister Masters had elevated our high school concert band to award-winning status, and so I was already nervous enough without Larry Throckmorton's not-so-friendly advice.

My audition was a nerve-racking experience. I had to perform, and I either knew how to play this goddamn rented cornet or I didn't. What the hell does a kid fresh out of sixth grade measure his musical acumen against? The only other people I had heard play the instrument were Louis Armstrong and Al Hirt. By comparison, I shouldn't even be allowed to blow air through the damn thing in public. Mister Masters sat beside me through the entire ordeal without uttering a sound. That didn't help. When it was over, all he said was, "Thank-you." I told him he was welcome. I had to wait two weeks to find out that I had made the junior high band.

Entering junior high school is a pretty big deal: the changing of classes, a different teacher for every subject, and the fast-paced subculture of the hallway between classes. Popularity and Peer Pressure trump Science and Math; Self-Conscious Pondering and Awkward Posturing topple History, English, and Health. The only time I was comfortable in my own skin was during band practice. I felt as if I belonged—as if I was a part of something larger than myself.

For the longest time, I didn't know if Mister Masters even knew my name. I usually knew my part, so there was no reason to single me out. One day, I heard it—my name. Mister Masters called out my name. He wanted me to know that he couldn't hear me and impressed upon me that my voice, musically speaking, was an essential part of this orchestra, so would I please let my presence be known? Mister Masters knew my name, and he wanted to hear my musical voice. What an ennobling moment that was.

One of the pieces Mister Masters had chosen for us to perform was The Triumphal March from Verdi's Aida. The first time I saw the score, my eyes bugged out at the mishmash of musical notes crammed onto every page. I wasn't even sure I had it right side up.

The music proved to be a daunting task. We worked on it for weeks without a pronounced improvement in our performance. We realized Mister Masters' patience was wearing thin, and at one point he halted our playing and shouted,

"You sound like a damn junior high school orchestra! Is that what you want? Do you want to sound like a damn junior high school orchestra?"

We sat staring straight ahead in breath-taking silence. Slowly, we began turning to look at one another. Not one of us in the damn junior high school orchestra wanted to sound like a "damn junior high school orchestra."

We rehearsed all year for the one concert held in the spring. One would think that rehearsing the same material for eight months would wear even the finest of fabrics to tattered cloth. However, Mister Masters made us look deeper into the music, exploring each passage for its particular significance and finding something new each time we played it. He taught us how to stop listening to the notes and hear the music, to turn our attention away from our individual selves, and to become an orchestra, albeit a damn junior high school orchestra.

When the time finally came for us to perform, the waiting backstage was a confusing mixture of nervous energy and confident mettle. We *knew* this music, and Mister Masters was directing our performance. In the waning minutes before we were to go on stage, I overheard one of the band members say that Mister Masters had been called in front of the school board because he had been too stern with a student in the high school band. The rumor was that he had slapped the student. I remember wondering if it was true and, if so, what the student had done to deserve it. Such was my devotion to Mister Masters.

The concert started at 7:30 sharp. We opened with Aaron Copland's "Fanfare for the Common Man." I couldn't believe what I was hearing. We had never sounded this good in practice. Something was happening in the performance that I don't think any of us understood, except Mister Masters.

As we finished the opening piece, the applause was so immediate and robust that we knew we didn't sound like a damn junior high orchestra. We followed with Sousa's The Stars and Stripes Forever, and the audience came out of their seats applauding before we had concluded the piece.

As the applause waned, Mister Masters said in a voice just loud enough for us to hear, "This is my last performance with you. I'm very proud of every one of you. Now let's give 'em all we got."

Everything in my world came to a single point of vital importance. It was a very long and confusing five seconds before the opening notes of 'Aida'. Mister Masters would be leaving, and this last performance took on a whole new significance. He raised his baton, and we played as if the survival of music depended upon it.

The performance had such strength and beauty, unlike anything I had ever experienced. I did not want it to end. As we held out the last note under the outstretched arms of Mister Masters, I cried. We cried—the whole damn junior high school orchestra cried. Off in the distance was the sound of a tremendous but futile applause and shouts of 'Encore!'...but there would be no encore...

After the concert was over and everyone was leaving or standing around chatting, I remained seated in my chair, immersed in the emptiness of the moment. I can't remember if I said goodbye or, more importantly, thank you to Mister Masters. I would like to think that I did. However, I can't imagine what words I would have used to express the feelings that, to this day, I am still sorting out.

One thing is clear: He taught me about passion. Not passion, as one uses the word these days to express a strong desire, but passion from its Latin root, 'pati'—*to suffer for*; a willingness to suffer that we may acquire an understanding of what it means to love something. For that, my dear Mister Masters, I am thankful beyond words.

To A Grievous Angel

It was around 3 in the morning of September 19th, 1973, when I heard the news. I was at some lame-ass party in L.A. with a couple of friends, and we had just drained the dregs from a bottle of Johnny Walker Black when Jack said,

"Well, now we've gone and done it—we've drunk all of their liquor."

"There is a whole keg of beer over there," Gary said, to which I replied,

"I can't drink that watered-down piss after drinking scotch all night."

It was then that a guy came on the radio and said that Gram Parsons was found dead in a Joshua Tree hotel room. Most of the people at the party had no idea who Gram was, but Jack, Gary, and I knew, and we just stood there staring at one another. 'Muscrat Love' came on the radio, and I said,

"Really? We're out of scotch, Gram's dead, and they are playing fucking Muscrat Love. I'm outta here."

The three of us left, went over to Jack's house, drank whiskey, and listened to Sweetheart of the Rodeo, Gilded Palace of Sin, Burrito Deluxe, and G.P. 'til the sun lit up the drizzle and smog of the brown skies above 'The City of Angels'.

That was fifty years ago, and Gram Parsons is still the kindling of a fire that burns within me. Thanks, Gram...

Breaking Even With Morianna

It was the shallowest of relationships, composed mainly of our own reflections, but, oh, wasn't she beautiful?

I always had a hunch about Morianna. A feeling that maybe she was deeper than she was letting on and that underneath all of that polish there was at least an eighth of an inch of real veneer. But then, I suffer from aesthetic Z-axis dyslexia—when looking at something beautiful, I see intelligence and emotional depth where there is none. This is partly because I want to discover a quality in someone that everyone else has overlooked. But also because, when it comes to beauty, I am shallow as hell and I need something to assuage the guilt.

After the initial self-deception wore off, I stopped looking for the deeper Morianna. There was no *deeper* Morianna. This left me disheartened and pissed off. Not at myself—at Morianna—she wasn't the person my imagination had designed her to be.

So there I was, with this beautiful, leaking balloon. I know this sounds selfish, and it is, but I also realize that Morianna was in it for Morianna. She was incapable of doing anything for any other reason than Morianna wanted to do it. She was a tautology: Morianna was the reason Morianna only did things for Morianna. It was beyond her internal gaze why anyone—me for example—would do anything that didn't meet her approval. And if I engaged in behavior outside her purview, she would get even. Not to be vicious. She thought getting even was proper behavior.

A few months into our relationship, I went to Big Sur camping with a friend. Morianna did not want me to go. She thought camping was childish. By the time I got home, she had taken off for L.A. with her friend, Molly. She hated L.A., and she wasn't exactly fond of Molly. She was getting even.

While she was in L.A., my friend, Steve, asked if I would play a gig with him at a ski lodge at Bear Mountain. I hated playing ski lodges, but the money was good, so I accepted Steve's offer. I tried several times to reach Morianna and concluded she was avoiding me, spelled g-e-t-t-i-n-g e-v-e-n.

When you play ski resorts, you have to play the sort of drivel that people who frequent ski lodges want to hear. They want music that reinforces their belief that life is good because they will it to be so. The patrons do not want to hear The Lonesome Death Of Hattie Carroll; they want to hear Rocky Mountain High. And whatever you do, do not play any "original" compositions. It only confuses them. They are not there to listen; they just want an air-freshener sound track under their inane conversation—a soft, familiar, unobtrusive background serving as musical wallpaper.

One evening, I received a phone call in the lounge. I knew it couldn't possibly be good news. When you are this well tucked away, it is rare that someone bothers to find you in order to tell you the good news.

It was Morianna.

"Hi. I guess you know by now that I'm in L.A."

"Yeah, I heard."

"It was a sort of, on the spur of the moment, thing."

"Well, I'm sure it took some thought."

"Excuse me?"

"Nothing."

"Anyway, I'm coming home early because I miss you."

"So, you and Molly aren't getting along?"

"We're getting along just fine. I miss you. Your brother told me you went to the ski lodge with Steven to make some money and flirt with the married chicks."

"Really? That's what my brother told you?"

"No, but I know why you really went. So, if I come back to San Francisco, will you come back too?"

"No Morianna. No, I won't. I committed to the gig, and I'm going to honor that commitment."

"You *hate* it there."

"Yeah, I do. So what?"

"What's really going on?"

"I'm playing out the rest of this month, Morianna. That's *what's really going on*."

"You're just doing that to get even with me."

"Well, it may have that benefit as well, but I'm really doing it because I told Steve I would and, frankly, I could use the money."

"I can't believe I'm ending my trip early and coming all the way back to San Francisco just because I miss you, and you're not willing to give up some stupid gig that you hate in order to be with me."

"It's all so simple for you, isn't it?"

"Yes. Yes, it is! Unlike you, I take this relationship seriously."

"We have no relationship, Morianna. We have never had a relationship. There was a distance between us when we met, and that same distance is still there today. And do you know why?"

"No, I don't. All I know is that I love you."

"*That* is why, Morianna. Because the only thing we know about each other... the only thing we have ever known about each other... is that we're in love, but I'm not so sure it is with each other. It's like a free pass to a season of concerts. We don't know or care who's playing. Cost isn't a consideration. All we know is that we get in free, so why not go? It was easy to commit to one another because it didn't really mean anything. We could talk for hours without a genuine disagreement because all we ever talked about was ourselves. It could be true that we *want* to love one another, Morianna, but the sad truth is, we don't know how."

I caught myself pausing for a moment to think about what I had just said, then continued. "Look, I'll see you in a couple of weeks. Maybe we can go to a play in the park or go hear a band that neither of us knows anything about. Who knows? It may turn out that we really do like each other. I hope so. But for now, let's cut our losses and trade in this thing we call love for an actual relationship."

"You're saying we should just be friends?"

"I didn't say that. I said, I would like for us to *try* to be friends."

"Well... I want more than that."

"I wish that were true, Morianna. I'll see you in a couple of weeks."

After I hung up, I realized I had just ended a love that never existed. I went outside into the dark and frozen silence, and I cried, although I wasn't sure why. It was so cold that my tears froze without falling. It seemed apropos.

When I came back to San Francisco, Morianna was gone. When she had come back from L.A. she stayed just long enough to pack her belongings and move to Seattle. She didn't even leave a note to say, "Goodbye."

IN OTHER WORDS

I miss Morianna. I was thinking this one night as I was crossing the Golden Gate Bridge, coming back into San Francisco. When I got to the tollbooth, I realized I didn't have any money. I pulled out my wallet to get the twenty-dollar bill I kept for emergencies, only to find it missing. Then I remembered... I had spent it on a 'Rolex' watch I bought from a street vendor down at the wharf. The damn thing never kept time and broke after a few weeks, but, oh, wasn't it beautiful?

J. R. BARNES

Her Most Precious Of Things

She had a locked glass case stocked full of them. There were cobalt blue cups and saucers, tiny little silver spoons, and plates with blue drawings of pastoral settings in wintertime. I knew the cups were not to be used as cups, nor the saucers, saucers; the spoons were much too small to serve any real purpose, but as for the plates, I really wanted to eat off of one of those plates. There was also a wide assortment of other mysterious objects that stirred my curiosity as to what purpose they may have once served. But she knew. She had a story about each item, and she loved to talk about 'her most precious of things'.

Whenever I visited my great-aunt's house, I would sit and stare into that glass case. My eyes were especially drawn to the tiny blue crystal objects that looked like tiny glasses, maybe large enough to hold a swallow or two of liquid something or other. No doubt she told me what they were, where they came from, who originally owned them, how she happened to have them, and why she kept them. I imagined each piece to be extremely valuable; but my favorite, the most valuable of all, was that small, deep blue lady's boot.

One day, she unlocked the case and let me hold the beautiful, cobalt blue lady's boot. She whispered, "Now don't tell your brother I opened the case for you, because then he will want me to open it for him. I don't open the case very often," she said, and then she whispered, "These are my most precious of things."

She held her hands cupped under mine as I carefully examined the delicate little boot. The light wove a jagged path through the contours of the blue glass and, at several curves and curls, reflected bright blue rays back into my eyes as I turned and rolled the piece between my fingers, hypnotizing myself. She spoke not a word, giving the magic its moment. When I looked up at her, she smiled an enduring smile and raised her cupped hands up to accept the piece, then gently put it back into the antique curio case, whispering, "s-h-h-h-h," as if we had broken a sacred museum rule. This is precisely how an object becomes priceless.

Many years later, I came home from California and was told she had died the year before. I was more than a little upset that no one had bothered to inform me of her passing. As I sat there quietly remembering her, the color blue brushed across my mind, and it transported me back in time to that locked glass case, her smiling child-like face, and 'her most precious of things'.

I asked, "Whatever became of her curio cabinet filled with all of those little glass things she loved so much?"

"What curio cabinet?" my brother asked.

"You know, the one in the kitchen she always kept locked," I said.

"Oh, that," he laughed. "I could never figure out why she kept that thing locked." Then he added, "I think one of the neighbors took the cabinet, and we tried to auction all that junk off, but no one wanted it, so we threw it all away. Why? Did you want that stuff?"

"I would like to have had one of the pieces," I said, recalling the precious little cobalt blue lady's boot.

My brother chuckled and said, "You can buy that crap anywhere."

Campbell's First Law of Failure
(As Told To Me By My Friend, Cary Campbell)
"Success is best measured by the failures endured."
- Cary Campbell

When I was eight years old, my Cub Scout Troop was in competition with another local Cub Scout troop, wherein each member of each group was to build a self-propelled rocket out of balsa wood and bring it to the Annual Cub Scout Gala to be held on Labor Day.

I was a young rocket scientist in those days, embarking on my first project, eager to demonstrate my scientific expertise.

My mother and I went to Shillito's, a local department store famous for its rocket propulsion department, and purchased the "Official Cub Scout Rocket Kit." It came in a deep-space blue box with a red, white, and blue rocket thrusting toward the moon pictured on the front. The road home was paved with fantasies straight from the pages of The Guinness Book of Cub Scout Records. There I was, on page 456:

Campbell, Cary: The first elastic-powered, propeller-driven balsa wood rocket to break the sound barrier and return to the launch site. Upon receiving the award, young Cary said, "My mom didn't help me, er nuthin'."

Once home, the project lay in pieces on the kitchen... I mean, the laboratory table. Trembling with anticipation, I opened the instructions; they unfolded like a roadmap to my future. I drew in a breath and held it as I read.

Easy-To-Follow Rocket Assembly Instructions

Step 1: Using your Official Wooden-Handled Single-Blade Stainless Steel Cub Scout Knife, carefully whittle the elongated block of balsa wood into a smooth cylinder shape, tapering one end into an aerodynamic nosepiece.

I released my breath and hung my head. I didn't have an *Official Wooden-Handled Single-Blade Stainless Steel Cub Scout Knife*. I also knew my mom wasn't about to take me back to Shillito's to purchase one.

I could feel my entry into the Guinness Book of Cub Scout Records slipping away. Not one to give up easily, but suffering a loss of zeal, I began looking around for a sharp kitchen knife. What I ended up using was an *Unofficial, Plastic-Handled, Free-With-A-Fill-Up, Serrated Sunoco Steak Knife.*

With each gouging stroke, my would-be rocket began to resemble a corncob. The aerodynamics of my rocket, as well as my hopes, were reduced to balsa chips. I had hit "rocket bottom."

I labored on half-heartedly, knowing my efforts were in vain. The final result of my disappointing efforts was a finless corncob, held together with black electrical tape wrapped in spirals, resembling a black and brown barber pole, with no hope of flight.

At the Cub Scout Gala, I held my pathetic entry close to me in a brown paper bag. It remained there.

This was the first of many failed attempts throughout the proceeding years where I left the remains of a perfect plan in a metaphorical brown paper bag held close to my side. One needn't put failure on display.

But failure doesn't consist of giving up; giving up is surrender. Failure is hard work. Failure is difficult, and its rewards are seeds concealed. I will, at times, surrender to perfection, but I will never again be afraid to fail.

A Father Departs

Some events can leave us with haunting memories; others can haunt us for want of them. My father left our family the day after Christmas, 1963. I have no recollection of the event.

Evidently, for the longest time, I didn't think about it. Years later, for some reason, I found myself wondering about the event, but it was as if several pages had been torn from that particular chapter.

I can recall losing my first kite and the vision of it diminishing to a tiny yellow dot as it disappeared into the infinite blue beyond. The aroma of my grandmother's basement is forever lodged in my mind. My great-aunt's delicate voice is as present in my ears as if she spoke to me a moment ago. The feel of my first sunburn, the taste of castor oil, and the forgiving smile on the face of my first grade teacher... all sorts of memories, good and bad, are available to me, but not the memory of my father leaving home—*the day after Christmas.*

When I informed my mother of this historical void, I found it diffi-cult to believe that his departure was as late as 1963. I was a sophomore in high school. Why did I think I was much younger? What does that mean? His leaving must have been a significant occasion with negative consequences, right? But actually, I think my life improved. I remember 1964 as a relatively auspicious time. Did his leaving somehow liberate me?

I know we didn't get along when he lived at home. He seemed so clumsy with me, and I with him. We were always so awkward around one another, and I became extremely self-conscious around him, so I was probably relieved when he finally left. I must have resented *him* for *our* not getting along; after all, I was a child; he was an adult, so the onus of responsible behavior was in his court. That doesn't relieve me of all responsibility. I could have tried harder to please him. But maybe at some point I simply gave up trying because I had come to believe he didn't much care for me. I don't know why I believed that; it was more of an emotional summary than a cognitive conclusion.

The long-term result of our broken relationship is that memories of my father are sparse; early childhood memories of him are almost nonexistent—sketchy, like the perfunctory scribbles of an artist not yet inspired. Adolescent memories are a little more involved, but no less confusing.

As of this writing, we have made amends. We have some sort of non-verbalized agreement to get along with one another. We carry it out to the consonant. We get along.

I suppose people are always searching their past or looking for clues about their future. Maybe these are two forms of the same desire—understanding the present. I don't much understand the present, in part because I don't understand or even remember a lot of the past. This, of course, means that I don't know who I was in one or am in the other. I think the poetic metaphor for all of this is "drifting."

I have been adrift for a long time, seeking and finding many ports. Some of them are geographic locations, some of them friends, lovers, or occupations, and there have been assorted chemical sidekicks along the way. I place no blame. I have reached the age where I accept full responsibility, if for no other reason than it is my only hope of finding my way home.

As a sailor adrift for most of his life, I need to face one more navigational possibility. There may not be a home for me. Home may be something that is created for us when we are very young and much more in need of it. And for those who were so fortunate as to have known it, they carry it with them always. But for those of us who were, at an early age, set adrift, every port is but a port of call.

And so, we are sailors. We know the streets. We know the people. We know the know. But, we are only home when we are sailing. Perhaps...

Note To My Father On Father's Day

Today being Father's Day, I thought I would listen to Bruckner's 7th Symphony and jot down a few notes. Bruckner's 7th Symphony has absolutely nothing to do with my relationship, or lack of one, with my father. I don't even know if he has heard said symphony, but, for some reason, it seems à propos. Perhaps it is because the music does not conjure up any memories of my father, and I wanted to be free of any particular emotional winds while sailing through this composition.

My father lives in Fort Myers, Florida. I would never have imagined this happening. I have always had this image of my father (created completely in his absence) as a man with no observable curiosity as it concerns The Sunshine State. You can throw in the Bahamas, Jamaica, and Cancun...the whole goddamn Caribbean Sea and the Gulf of Mexico.

I simply cannot visualize my father basking in the boiling boredom of the noonday sun, pondering nothing but the final arc of his existence as he stares at an illusory horizon.

Knowing my father, as only I could imagine him, he is incapable of such an existence. As a result, I am forced to believe he living in this season-less, kiln-like environment against his will. Something, I know not what, has intervened and whisked him away. He is making the most of it, to be sure. He wouldn't complain. That is simply not part of my imaginary father's constitution.

The truth, as near as it can be known, is that I don't know my father at all. I have never, but for rare occurrences, really known the where-abouts of my father, literally or figuratively. He has always been, but for a son's imagination, absent.

But, this being Father's Day, I wish him the best... well, maybe not the best; I hope it is always one degree hotter than he prefers. It would please me if, as he stares out over the Gulf of Mexico pondering things, he takes pause to think of his not so imaginary son. That would be nice, but I'll never know, so I'll just imagine it to be so.

Happy Father's Day Dad... whatever you ponder... wherever you are.

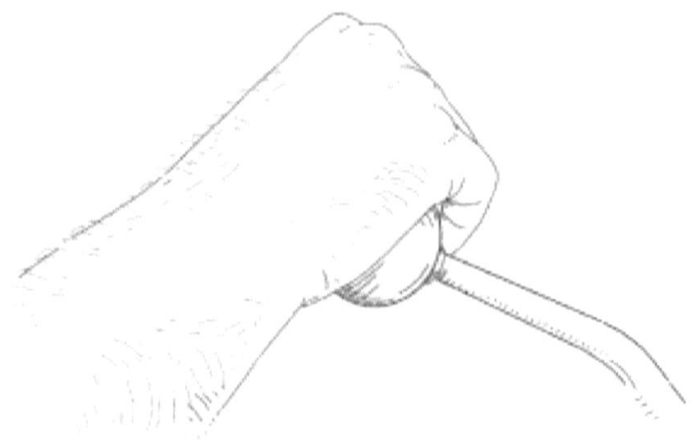

For Uncle David

Uncles come in a variety of sizes, shapes, and degrees of personal significance. But you—you were a giant of a man to me. When I was a child, you always spoke to me as if I were your buddy. You were never condescending or paternalistic. While doling out wisdom with a sense of humor, you were always ready to point out the irony of things and the bewitchery of illusion.

You once stood in front of me and said, "I look pretty big to you, don't I?" I agreed. You took out a cigarette, lit it, and asked, "I look even bigger now, don't I?" I couldn't help but nod in genuine agreement. "See how easily you are fooled?" he said. "I'm just the same guy with a cigarette in his mouth."

I remember when I turned 15; you told me it was time for me to learn how to drive, and you insisted I learn in your manual shift, '57 Ford. I told you I would prefer to learn on an automatic. You said, "No, you wouldn't; there's a difference between driving and steering.'" I somehow knew you were talking about more than just driving a car.

You always smiled when you saw me. I wonder if you knew how welcome that made me feel. You would shake my hand when saying 'goodbye'; I wonder if you knew how grownup that made me feel. I don't think you had any idea how much you exemplified self-respect and personal dignity to me. On the one hand, I wish I had told you how much you meant to me, but on the other, I think you would much rather have me carry it forward by standing as tall as you stood and winking at the troubles of the world with that 'David Sparks' twinkle in the eye. I'll try, Uncle David—I'll try.

A Memory In Passing

Bob's smile would always greet me halfway, as I came strolling down Paint Street on any given day that I happened along. As I came within earshot, he would ask, "Where have you been?" not really expecting an answer; it was his way of saying, 'I've missed you'. Should there be an empty chair at the small table outside Schlegel's Coffee House, I would sometimes join him, his friend Bill, and whoever else was present. There was always a discussion in progress, and sometimes I felt as if I were interrupting, but he had a marvelous talent for making me feel welcome without missing a beat in the conversation. He would turn those piercing eyes toward me, looking for a reaction to someone's (usually Bill's) comment, and eventually, he would find a way to pull me into whatever was being discussed—usually a quibble between Bob and Bill's differing views of an assortment of subjects. Bill, leaning back, arms folded, speaking his mind in a straightforward, matter-of-fact style; Bob, cigarette in one hand, coffee in another; legs crossed, revealing yet another pair of flamboyant socks, smiling that whimsical smile while preparing his repartee.

We had been Majestic Theater board members together, and he was always a significant source of encouragement and support for me, even when I was the lone dissenter.

He had worked for my father and somehow knew that my father and I had a strained relationship. He wanted me to know that he held my father in high regard and relayed several stories about him, giving me a little more insight into a man that has always been somewhat of a mystery to me.

One night, during a Majestic Board meeting, I received a text saying my father had died. I sat staring at my phone, unable to grasp the gravity of the moment. Finally, I excused myself and stepped outside. Bob, sensing something was wrong, followed me out.

"Are you alright?" he asked.

"My father just passed away," I said.

His face drained pale, his eyes welled with tears, and he placed his hands on my shoulders and wept. It was the strangest feeling; me standing there dry-eyed, composed, and wooden; Bob crying the tears I could not find.

That is the Bob Etling I knew. S'long Bob, I will miss you...you and those damn socks.

Note From A Musical Hermit

It is March 2021, and I haven't had a 'gig' in quite some time, and not just because of COVID-19. I booked only three gigs in 2019, telling myself I was tired of playing the same songs to the same people in the same venue(s)...but it is a shaved truth. I could have, at any time, changed any or all of those variables—I chose not to. So, upon reflection, I have to conclude:

It is not the songs. I love the songs I perform. I am always finding new ways to play the old songs, searching for songs that have long fallen out of favor, or writing original songs. Admittedly, I rarely perform popular songs, not because I dislike them but because they reek of familiarity. Therefore, I either do not possess the talent to faithfully duplicate them or I lack the creativity to free them from their conventional groove.

It is not the audience. I truly appreciate anyone who takes time out of their life to sit and listen to my musical offerings. I hold in the hollows of my heart a reserved space for those who know me and take the time to show up. It is so rewarding to find a friend or fellow musician seated out front every once in a while. It feels like validation of some sort of thing or another.

It is not the venue. I appreciate the opportunity to play on every stage on which I have stood... (or sat). I have, with rare exception, been gracious to my host and excited whenever they ask me to return. True, I do not relish being an atmospheric musician or human jukebox; I like venues where I can share a rapport between songs with the audience. However, I realize most gigs are not of that nature. Occasionally, with the help of friends like John Victor and a revolving cast of fellow musicians, poets, and artists, friends, and various hosts, we put on a show. It is these outings that I have enjoyed most of all. So, it isn't the venue that counts as much as the presentation. And so I feel a bit ashamed and should apologize for having once or twice blamed the venue for a lackluster performance.

It is not the songs, the audience, or the venue that have kept me from performing. It is because I have let the shine wear off. I have allowed a certain cynicism to creep into my performing soul, and I tried to veneer it over with a showman's smile. But after a year and a half of self-imposed musical hermitage, I find I miss the very things I sought refuge from: the songs, the audience, and the venues.

I have no idea when or even if I will begin 'playing out' again. But I want to say this to the folks who make being a musician such a joy: I want you to know, I miss you...

Searching Through A Second Movement By Beethoven

I have heard this so many, many times before—and still I return to it, listening for something I have not heard.

Listening for something I know I have not heard.

I know this music. Those interlacing harmonies flowing through my being; my heart beating to the Allegretto tempo... and yet, there is always something calling out to me from between the notes, saying, "Listen...listen closer. Do you hear it? Listen..."

Listening to Beethoven I am grounded by what I know by heart, and lifted by what my heart can touch but cannot grasp...

Isn't this just like a conversation with you?

I have come to know, almost to the verb, your response to any gathering of thoughts that may part my lips—but still, I seek your reply.

Why?

The answer lies in the beauty of the voice.

I am listening for the soul of the singer.

IN OTHER WORDS

I am listening for what I cannot grasp, and yet, have come to know by heart.

I am listening for Beethoven.

I am listening for you.

On My Way To Becoming Rick

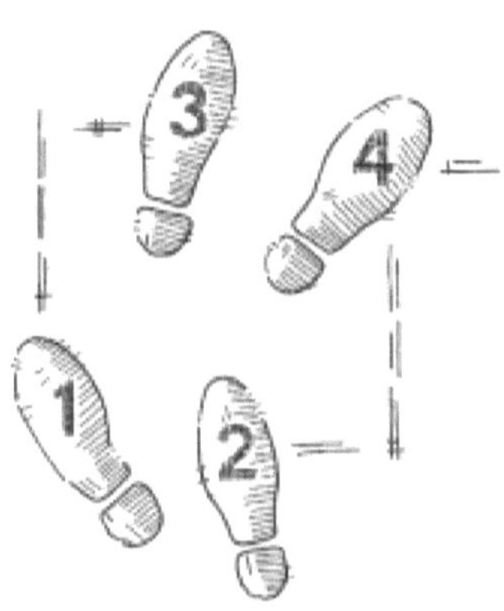

The Killer Instinct

When I was young and too brash by half, I developed a tradition of getting my ass beat on a regular basis. Having grown tired of being on the losing end of the scrap, I asked my father to teach me how to box. He said he wished there was a way to teach me how to hold my tongue, but we both knew that wasn't going to happen.

He began by telling me, "It's a dance, son. The best dancer wins. It's all about the dance."

He showed me the boxer's stance, relaxed, confident, and fluid. Stay on the balls of your feet. Step and drag, step and drag, forward, back, and to the side, step and drag. Never cross your feet; stay out of your opponent's 'power range'.

He taught me the moves—some defensive, some offensive—and what each could be called upon to do and when I should use them. There was a series of punches and jabs designed for deflecting, stinging, stunning, wounding, and finally, going in for the kill—the knockout punch.

I remember saying, "This is an awful lotta stuff to remember."

He replied, "Don't try to remember it; you'll get killed. Practice it until you know it, and then work on the mental dance. Watch for the punch your adversary tries to hurt you with—that is the punch he fears the most. You cannot show any signs of hesitation or doubt, and keep a constant lookout for the fear in your opponent's eyes; and above all, you have to develop a killer instinct. That is to say, you have to know when to move in for the kill."

My father's lessons were not an immediate success. I was pummeled many times while posing in a boxer's stance. When I eventually won my first fight, it turned out to be my last. I had my opponent backed up against the wall, a look of terror in his eyes. He swung at me with a wild punch and missed. This was it—time to move in for the kill. I leaned in, cocked my arm back, tightened my fist, and... I just couldn't do it.

He lowered his head and slid to the ground in shameful defeat—I knew exactly how he felt. I reached out, pulled him to his feet, and I *apologized*.

Later, I explained to my father that I lacked the killer instinct, and without it, fighting was just a defensive chore. And, while I believe in defending myself, I take little pleasure in 'winning' the fight.

I thought I wanted to know how to box. As it turns out, it was the dance itself that fascinated me. "It's all about the dance," my father told me. Come to think of it, what isn't?

Listening For The Moon

When I was much smaller than I am now and the heavens were much larger by measure, my family went vacationing at the northern tip of Ohio, overlooking the vast reach that is Lake Erie. Late one evening, my father and I were standing at the water's edge beneath a moonless sky filled with stars.

I looked up at my father and asked, "Where is the moon?"

He replied, "Tonight is the new moon."

I looked at the sky... nothing.

"So then, where is the moon?" I asked again.

He explained the moon is not visible when it is new.

My brow lowered, and I gave the slightest shake of my head. "What's so 'new' about it if it isn't there?" I asked.

"Oh, it's there; you just can't see it," my father reassured me.

"How do you know it's there if no one can see it?" I challenged.

"You can hear it," he said. "Listen..."

All I could hear was the rhythmic sound of waves crashing against the shore.

"Do you hear it?" he asked.

Then, to the beat, he explained to me how the moon's invisible gravity affects our planet's tides and how verification comes in many forms.

And so tonight, under another new moon, in yet another blue yonder, I am searching through the vastness of a different darkness—looking, listening, and waiting—waiting for the invisible to reveal itself to me.

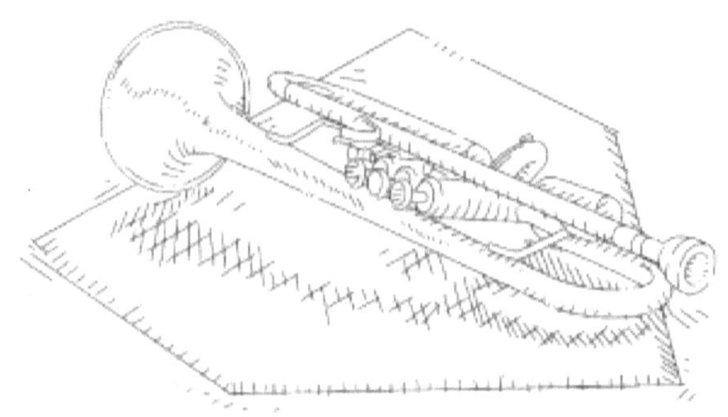

Passing, On The American Pastime

"Sports build character!" That's what they told me, over and over and over again. And I believed them. Of course, I had no idea what character was, but never mind; I was pretty sure *they* knew what character was, and *they* said sports built it, so...

Like every other kid in my neighborhood, I wanted to play baseball. Not so much to build character, but simply because it looked like fun. My parents did not prod or encourage me to participate in sports. In fact, my father hated sports. He only played catch with me once, and by once, I mean one throw of the ball. I threw him the ball, and he misjudged its trajectory so badly that it flew over his head and rolled down the hill into the woods. That was the end of that. So I guess I never really played catch with my father; I played throw.

By the time I was old enough to play ball with the older boys, I didn't really understand anything as far as the actual playing of the game. I didn't own a baseball glove, so I had to borrow one from the opposing team when they came up to bat. It was always a right-hander's glove, and I, being left-handed, had to catch and throw with the same hand, so I couldn't even pretend that I knew what I was doing. I learned to bat by watching other people and following their example, so I batted right-handed—yet another conspicuous display of my ineptitude.

To help put this experience into (painful) perspective, here is a list of some of the older guys I played baseball with when I was 10 years old:

A future Rookie of the Year quarterback for the Cincinnati Bengals.

A future three-time letterman with the Ohio State Buckeyes football team.

A future Olympic diver.

The son of, quoting Sports Illustrated, "One of the best tight ends in the history of the Pittsburgh Steelers."

With these guys in the mix when we were choosing sides, I didn't really mind getting picked last, but I did mind those times when I didn't get picked at all. This gave a whole new meaning to the phrase, 'No one is better than me.'

These guys were all about winning. Fuck character. There was no such thing as losing gracefully. They wouldn't hesitate to send me home for a dropped ball or tell me to step into a pitch and get 'beaned'—you know, 'take one for the team'. Willfully getting 'beaned' by a little league pitcher my age is a sacrifice. Willfully getting 'beaned' by a future Rookie of the Year quarterback for the Cincinnati Bengals is suicide. The first time he 'beaned' me, I couldn't move my left arm for two days.

I learned through trial and error (mostly error) to play the game, but I was never very good at it, although, win or lose, I always had fun playing. But it got to the point where I was too much of a liability and was finally told I couldn't play because, 'Losing isn't any fun'. So as far as the whole character-building thing is concerned, I still don't know what the hell that was all about.

Anyway, I sort of fell out of favor with sports in general and baseball in particular. It was, and still is, 'just a game' to me. You know, as in a baseball *game*. I have been informed that anyone who holds this particular opinion isn't really much of a fan. The folks making up M.L.B., the N.F.L' or the N.B.A. are obsessed with winning at all costs. "Winning isn't everything; it's the *only* thing" is perhaps the most famous quote in sports history. How sad. To me, the real value of sports is that it reflects the values of our culture within the framework of a game. Sort of like the Romans watching the disintegration of their civilization down on the floor of the Coliseum.

I walked home crying from several of those neighborhood games, feeling like an All-American Failure as an American kid. But knowing I wasn't any good at baseball and probably never would be wasn't why I was crying. I was crying because I was left out—left out of a *game*.

Well, one can only wear that mantle for so long, so I decided to spend those afternoons practicing my cornet instead of playing baseball, and, lo and behold, I discovered an America that included me—but that's another essay.

A Christmas Gift

I remember well the long night of my twelfth Christmas Eve. I lay awake, watching the snow silently fall outside my bedroom window. 'How perfect is this?' I thought... and yet, something was missing. In a few hours, it would all begin—the hustle and bustle of Christmas morning.

I had always had trouble falling sleep the night before Christmas. I would lie awake, writhing with anticipation, until exhaustion stole me away. But this year, the tossing and turning was much more disturbing. This wasn't the jitters; this was anxiety. I wasn't looking forward to Christmas morning; I was dreading it. All the gift-giving seemed so pointless. Why was everyone giving each other gifts? What did it all mean? Why was it mandatory? How can a 'gift' be mandatory? Everything seemed upside-down.

Around four in the morning, I wrapped myself in a blanket, opened my bedroom window, and snuck out of the house into an evening lit deep blue by moonlight gleaming off the crystalline snow. As I made my way through the fresh-fallen powder, the faint, self-conscious voice of my footsteps broke the evening's perfect silence.

At the end of the street was an ancient Indian burial mound. An old, hollowed-out tree sat at the base with an arched opening just wide enough for me to squeeze comfortably inside.

Cocooned, feeling but the slightest shiver, I quietly eavesdropped on the world, watching the moonlit snowflakes lilt toward earth, each flake coming softly to rest as if settled by an unseen hand, and listening into the silences, as a bird must, for any disturbance of the hush.

I don't remember drifting off to sleep, but when I awoke, the sun was breaking over the horizon, reflecting a warm orange glow off the pure white blanket of snow. I heard a cardinal singing in the distance, and a woodpecker was busy drumming on the very tree I was nestled in. I could have remained there all day, but I had obligations elsewhere.

Walking back home alongside my barely visible footsteps leading in the other direction, I thought to myself, 'I need to give more thought to the meaning of the word *gift*.'

Sneaking back in through the bedroom window and slipping into bed, no one the wiser, I drifted off to sleep.

I awoke to the sound of my brother's voice, saying, "C'mon, get up; we're unwrapping the Christmas presents."

I watched as everyone unwrapped their gifts and remembered my mother telling me, "The true meaning of a gift is in the giving." How true that is! We are each of us given the gift of wonder, and we need only to unwrap it to give it back to the world.

We Can't Stay Long

"Hi, Jim. Is that your boy?" the butcher said as my father and I entered Schmitt's Meat Market one windy October morning.

"Yeah, this is my boy, Say 'hello' to Mister Schmitt, son."

I gave a single nod of my head, 'Hello'.

"Your dad and his friend Bernie used to come in here begging for free wieners when they were about your age. You remember that, Jim?"

"I sure do, Mister Schmitt," my father said.

Mister Schmitt handed me a free hot dog and said, "Like father, like son." I accepted the cold dog, although I wasn't sure what I was supposed to do with it. "Do you ever see Bernie anymore, Jim?"

"It's been a while," Dad replied.

"I hear he's still livin' in that run-down apartment on Water Street. You know the one I'm talkin' about?"

"Yeah."

"You know his son drowned?" Mister Schmitt asked while assuming my dad already knew.

"I heard something about that. When was that?"

"Oh, let's see... been about a year or so ago." Mister Schmitt shook his head and added, "He was trying to swim across the Scioto River. There's talk he was high on something."

I knew it was coming—that look. I glanced quickly at my father, and there it was—the expression that brooked no comment.

"Last I heard, Bernie's not doing very well," Mister Schmitt said. "Poor soul. That boy meant everything to him."

My father's expression softened as he continued to look at me.

There was a moment of silence.

"What can I do for you today, Jim?"

"Let me have a pound of hamburger, a pound of bologna, and a pound of wieners... Make that two pounds of wieners—one for me, one for Bernie."

"Atta boy," Mister Schmitt said with a wink.

On our way out the door, my dad said, "Thank the man for the wiener, son."

"Thanks for the hot dog," I said, eyes forward, out the door.

As we walked to the car, dad asked me, "Aren't you going to eat your wiener?"

"Raw? Are you kidding me? And I really wish you would stop calling them 'wieners.'"

"They're already cooked; they're just cold. You've never eaten a cold wiener?"

I faked a gag and handed him the cold dog. He ate the thing in three bites, licked his fingers, and said, "When I was a kid, that's the only way I would eat 'em."

"That's disgusting."

"Do you mind if we make a quick stop?" he asked. "I want to drop off a pack of these wieners to Bernie."

I shrugged my shoulders.

We pulled up in front of an ash-gray building butted up between two other ash-gray buildings on a block lined with ash-gray buildings, all joined together as if to hold each other up. My mother had often told me to avoid this street when walking downtown. 'Nothing but drunks, thieves, and prostitutes hanging around in pool halls, bars, and sleazy flophouses,' my mother would say. Looking out the passenger-side window, I saw an old man in a dirty blue bathrobe, wearily looking out of a raised second-story window. When he saw me looking up at him, he flipped his cigarette butt at our car.

"Come on, I want you to meet Bernie," my dad said.

"Do I have to?" I asked.

"C'mon," he ordered.

The entrance to the building was a dark passageway, like the opening of a cave. Empty hinges gave evidence of a missing door, not that it seemed to matter, there was nothing to steal except empty wine bottles still in their brown paper bags, cigarette butts smoked down to the filter, and an assortment of crumpled, stained, and deteriorating trash.

Tramping through the rubbish, we came to a door that had obviously not been latched for years. The edge of the door's threshold rubbed against the floor as my father tried to push it open. He laughed a nervous half-laugh, grabbed the doorknob, lifted the drooping door up, and swung it open. Once inside, as he struggled to close it, I thought to myself, 'Why bother?'

Inside the dimly lit hallway, my father managed to find a light switch and flicked it, but nothing happened, so naturally he flicked it several more times. Apartments lined both sides of the dark hallway, their numbers painted on the doors in haphazard fashion.

Straight ahead was a set of stairs, and as we made our way up, the creak of each step emphasized the silence we had broken. I remember feeling oddly sorry for anyone who had to climb those stairs in order to get home.

When we arrived at the first landing, my father hesitated.

"I think it's the third door on the left," he whispered.

I wasn't sure why he was whispering, but I whispered back, "Okay."

He tapped on the door, and we stood there waiting... Just as I was hoping no one would answer, my father knocked a little louder... and we waited even longer. I think my father was on the verge of feeling some sort of congratulatory satisfaction at having made an attempt to see Bernie, when the door eased open, and there stood a curve of a man who looked much older than my father. He mumbled something or other that ended with my father's name, and then, before inviting us in, he apologized for his unkempt appearance. As we stepped into the cramped, stale, and poorly lit apartment, my father said,

"Well, we can't stay long. We were just in the neighborhood, and—"

Bernie closed the squeaky door behind us and said, "Jim, it's good to see you. Is that your boy?"

"Yeah. Say hello to Bernie, son."

I nodded hello, and Dad led me deeper into the dim interior, saying to Bernie, "We really can't stay too long."

Dad and Bernie each ate a cold hot dog and shared a broken conversation about half-remembered pieces of a past long gone. Bernie was almost apologetic in his mention of the loss of 'Junior', as if he didn't want to burden my father. My father turned to me for a reaction. The lowering of my eyes was my only contribution to the discussion.

I sat in an old, dusty chair, watching particles of dust dance in the beam of sunlight streaming in through the dirty windows. I wondered how a book would read, starting with Bernie and Dad, each chewing on a wiener while leaving Schmitt's Meat Market for the last time, and concluding here, years later, two old friends, chewing on their wieners in this squalid dump.

Dad pushed his chair back and said to Bernie, "I've got to get my boy back home. I'll try to stop by again... sometime soon. You take care of yourself, Bernie. If there's anything you need, let me know."

Bernie thanked Dad for the wieners and said how good it was to see him again. When he looked at me, his parched lips curled in an imitation of a smile. I remember thinking, *He has forgotten how to smile.*

As we left the building and stepped out into the bright light of the busy street, it was as if the world had been on hold and was just now starting to twirl again. I looked back over my shoulder at the darkened doorway from which I had just emerged, and I said to my father,

"Dad, is it okay if I never go back there with you again?"

I'm not sure he understood what I was really trying to say. Neither do I.

Almost A Mormon

I can remember searching for some sort of religious foundation at a very early age. Like all first steps taken by a child, it was a clumsy and haphazard venture concerned more with footing than destination.

I grew up with an abundance of faith but very little belief. I knew, to quote Alan Watts, there was "some sort of something somewhere." It was the particulars that puzzled me. I leaned toward a Christian belief (no real surprise since that was the only belief system to which I had been exposed), and I thought there were only two Christian religions from which to choose, Protestant and Catholic, and my mother was quite obstinate in her insistence that Catholicism was the wrong choice.

I knew nothing of the Jewish faith. I thought it was a dead religion—Moses as Ptolemy, Jesus as Copernicus— kind of deal. Growing up, I believed the word Jew was a verb until I was ten years old. I say this not as some ignorant attempt at humor; I say it because that was the only way I heard the word used. Buddhists, Muslims, Hindus? Never heard of 'em. Baptists, Methodists, and Lutherans—I tried all three.

The Baptists were too loud, always shouting about something or other. God as an angry dad; us as naughty children; and, "You just wait 'til you come home to your Father!"

The Methodists were too quiet, and always so damn polite. Attending church was like visiting a corporate board meeting: Father, Son, and Holy Ghost, religion by committee. We had no say, but there was plenty of whispering.

I couldn't quite figure out what the Lutherans believed, but my best friend was a Lutheran, and that was enough for me, for a while anyway.

By the age of fifteen, I was none of the above. I had given up on religion and was on the verge of tipping backward into Hell when a certain Elder Richards from the Church of Jesus Christ of Latter-day Saints came a-knocking on our door. I was the only one home, and, being somewhat bored, I invited him in, more to taunt him than to listen. But he knew his calling well and made a good showing of himself, addressing my objections, questions, and doubts. So convincing was his presentation that I invited him back to meet my mom.

"You did what?" she asked. "You invited a Mormon into our home?" She was not happy. When I informed her further that I had invited him back to meet her, she stared that stare that only mothers stare, and asked rhetorically, "What is wrong with you?" After some cajoling, she agreed to meet him. In summary, he won her over as well.

After a couple of meetings and a few services, I was ready to be baptized as a Mormon. I knew full well what that meant: no more coffee, tea, alcohol, or tobacco. 'The perfect time to quit,' I thought. I prepared diligently for the big day. We had rehearsed the baptismal ceremony, and I knew that at the moment of complete submersion in the holy water, I would be washed clean and would be filled with God's grace.

There were about ten of us to be baptized on that glorious day. We were each told to disrobe and put on the thin, full-length white gown they had provided. I stood in line, feeling full of holy anticipation. Then, step-by-step, I waded into the baptism pool. The water came up to about mid thigh and was a tad on the chilly side. Two men, one on either side of me, grabbed my arms, leaned me back, said their say, and pushed me under water. I came up feeling rejuvenated. Everything they told me I would feel, I felt. I walked out of the pool and turned around to witness the baptisms of those behind me.

Into the water waded the cutest little teenage girl I had ever laid eyes on. I couldn't believe she had been standing behind me the whole time, and I hadn't even noticed her. The two men did their duty and pushed her under the baptismal water to her salvation. How lovely.

The trouble started when she came back up. There she stood, draped in the world's largest wet T-shirt, clinging to her ripe and naked body, leaving nothing to my young and inflamed imagination.

My body parts reacted immediately. My eyes widened and simultaneously moistened so that I wouldn't have to blink. With an audible gasp, my lungs sucked in a massive amount of air to supply my brain with enough oxygen to maintain consciousness. This required my heart to operate at a pressure and pace it had never even approached before. My entire chest cavity heaved forth in response, and my blood vessels widened to accommodate the torrent of blood gushing out of the aorta of my jackhammering heart. Immense quantities of blood rushed into the rapidly filling reservoir of my flaccid phallus, which rose to the occasion, hoisting the front of my baptismal gown high enough to expose my knees.

I remember thinking, 'What in the name of John the Baptist is wrong with me? Here I am, not even sixty-seconds saved, standing before the entire congregation, visibly lusting after the Lord's most recent convert. You better dunk me again, the first one didn't take.'

Then a familiar voice inside of me broke through, as it has on so many occasions. It informed me that what I was feeling was perfectly normal; only the circumstances were odd. These feelings are to be celebrated, not condemned, and that sex, like food and music, is cause for great joy.

I vowed to never again embrace a religion or spiritual order that did not venerate sexuality.

I was only a Mormon for about a minute and seven seconds, probably some kind of record. I left the ceremonies and never returned to the Mormon Church. As a matter of fact, I have shunned membership in any church since that reverent day. Not because I am ashamed of what happened, but rather because I am not.

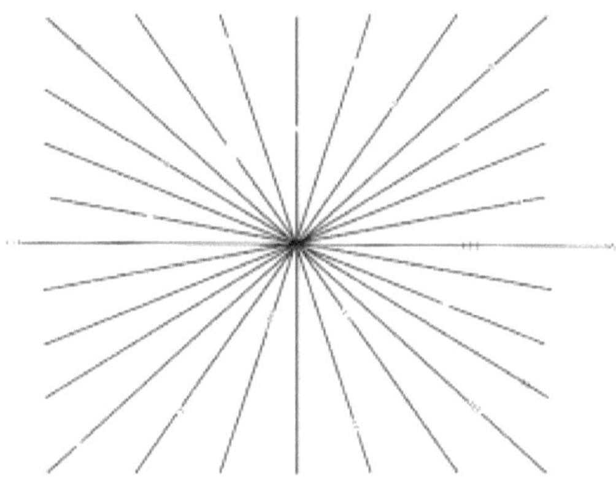

The Geometry Of Pam

If it hadn't been for my next-door neighbor, I would have failed geometry. Part of my problem (and it was *my* problem) was my juvenile cheeky posture toward all of my teachers, and my geometry teacher in particular.

He was a wiry little man with a thin, nasal voice and a manic obsession with mathematics. He would read us the different rules of geometry as if they were newly discovered sexual positions from the Far East—math was his Kama Sutra. His world was a world of numbers. Numbers were his whole life. He ate numbers. He dreamed about numbers. All he ever talked about was numbers. His wife was a mathematical equation, and his children derivatives of a common function.

The only thing that differentiated him from a computer was the fact that he picked his nose—his very prominent nose. This constant burrowing of both nostrils was carried out with all the nonchalance of someone clearing their throat, and being a man who spoke through his schnozz, that is precisely what he was doing. He had, in all probability, descended from a long line of nose pickers. His father was a nose picker, his grandfather was a nose picker, and his son was doomed to be a nose picker. But genetic disposition aside, his nose-picking distracted me from the task at hand, which was learning just enough geometry to pass.

It seems as if the cards were stacked against me. When his adenoidal drone or nasal excavation weren't distracting me, Pam was. Pam was the loveliest creature the Good Lord ever placed in a geometry class. She was a perfect piece of geometry. If there was an equation that could get me between those parallel lines that ran from the floor to her seat, Ol' Booger Nose wasn't going to teach it to me.

"Two parallel lines never converge," he informed us one day.

Pam raised her hand and asked, "Didn't Einstein say that there was a point at which parallel lines would finally meet?"

"Well, Pamela, that was part of a much larger theory."

I stared at the fold in her skirt, understanding Einstein's theory perfectly.

He twanged on: "Einstein theorized that if two lines, running parallel, stretched out eternally through the curved universe, there is a point at which they would meet."

I gazed at what was to me, the eternal distance between the base of her feet and the crease in her skirt, knowing that Einstein was right. Man-O-Man, if I could only behold that most holy of places.

"So then it is possible that parallel lines do eventually meet," she asked.

OH GOD, PAM! I was drooling now. Take me into the grasp of your perfect geometry and show me the possibilities of your universe! Take me to that point where only my imagination has dared to soar. Then beyond! Beyond the reach of my imagination and numbers. Teach me, Pam, right here on the floor, in front of God and everybody. What the hell is a classroom for, anyway?

Oh, Dear Lord, I am l-o-s-i-n-g it! I've got to get a grip before I commit a horrible crime against nature in the name of science.

"Well, anything is possible, Pamela," he replied with one finger in his nose.

Oh, all ye powers that be, grant me that possibility.

"Do you believe it's true?" Pam asked him.

WHAT ARE YOU ASKING HIM? Who cares what he believes? What about me? Can't you see I'm dying of curiosity? God, I'm slobbering! I wonder if anyone has noticed. FUCK THEM! Who cares? Oh Dear Mother of God, don't let me lose all self-control!

"Well, Pamela," he professed, "Staying within the elementary discipline of this class, I would have to say—"

"OH SHUT UP, BOOGER NOSE!" I blurted out. "I believe it, Pam. I do; I swear I do...

Oh, look down upon me, Sweet Jesus. What have I done?

The silence that fell upon the classroom began to permeate the universe. Everyone was staring at me in embarrassed disbelief. 'The Nose' came over and whacked me on the head with a ruler. That broke the silence. For that, I was grateful.

"Go to the principal's office at once and wait for me," he instructed.

As I walked down the hall, I could hear the wheels of the universe beginning to grind again. 'The world isn't ready for Einstein's theory,' I thought.

I had to stay after school and compose a blackboard dissertation composed of six words, repeated 1000 times—I WILL NOT DISRUPT CLASS AGAIN—a relatively minor and altogether mild punishment not completely void of justice.

To be honest, there was one more very important consideration to examine concerning my inability to absorb geometry. I, for the life of me, couldn't figure out why geometry was important. Of what benefit was this subject to my everyday life? In other words, I had not been exposed to the mystery of it all. It just seemed like a pile of equations, piled upon piles of equations, reaching outward toward nowhere.

Fortunately, my next-door neighbor, having accepted a bribe from my mother, took pity on me and introduced me to the wonder of it all.

Pam rarely, if ever, spoke to me, but she would occasionally give way to an all-knowing, if somewhat cautious, smile. The magic inherent in the world of mathematics and its sometimes unorthodox interpretations still intrigues me, and I look back now with an incremental increase in respect for Ol' Booger Nose, his passion for numbers, and his dedication to teaching, not to mention the exponential rise in my appreciation for the Geometry of Pam.

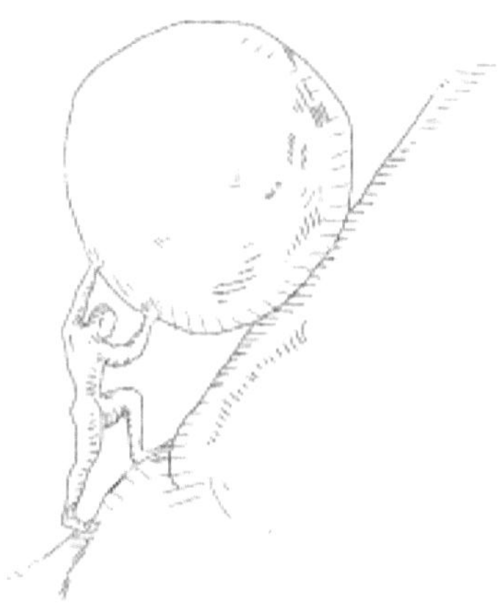

Phillip Of Purgamentum

I am sure you have heard the expression, 'Follow your heart.' My friend Erin scoffs at this sentiment, saying it is an elitist view of life.

According to Erin, and I quote: "Not everyone has the opportunity to cast off their responsibilities and go dashing about chasing their dream. For some folks, to dream is to invite despair. Who dreams of cleaning up the trash, emptying the trash, collecting the trash, and disposing of the trash?"

To which I responded, "Following your heart may have nothing to do with your job, economic status, social standing, or zip code. Quite the contrary, it may require a total abandonment of such concerns."

I also believe *she* is being elitist in her opinion concerning the value of the work some people do, e.g., cleaning up the trash, emptying the trash, collecting the trash, and disposing of the trash.

During a break from my undergraduate studies in philosophy at Ohio University, I received a valuable lesson in the art of following one's heart. I was working as a janitor in Morrill Tower Dormitory at Ohio State University. My boss, Phillip, had a PhD in philosophy from Columbia University. One day, I asked him what he planned on doing with his degree. The following is, as best I can recall, the rest of the conversation.

Phillip: What do you mean when you ask, 'What am I planning to do with my degree?'

Me: You know, are you actively looking for a job somewhere?

Phillip: I have a job.

Me: I mean one related to your degree.

Phillip: This job *is* related to my degree.

Me: How is being a janitor related to your degree in philosophy?

Phillip: I studied philosophy because I find it the most interesting of subjects. This job allows me to pursue my continued interest in philosophy, and it is in keeping with my personal philosophy as concerns the purpose and meaning of a good life.

Me: I'm not sure I understand...

Phillip: When I come to work, everything is in disarray. I am in charge of returning it to a semblance of order. At day's end, I turn around and look at what I have done, and I am pleased; things are, for lack of a better expression, better than I found them.

Me: But then you come back tomorrow, and things are a mess again.

Phillip: Yes. What is your point?

Me: Everything you have done is undone.

Phillip: Yes. Then I redo it.

Me: Isn't that kind of pointless?

Phillip: Give me an example of something that, once done, remains finished; something that remains forever unscathed; something that doesn't require any maintenance or preservation.

I took a pause and thought for a moment...

Phillip: Having a little trouble? Consider this: Everything falls apart. That is the nature of things. You yourself will fall apart. Everything you accomplish will either break or die, be forgotten, rust away, or become irrelevant. In time, the earth itself will turn to cinder—a lifeless speck of solid ash speeding aimlessly through the ever-expanding void. What I do here is simply to maintain a semblance of order in the interim.

Me: Damn... that's depressing.

Phillip: Is it? Why do you find it depressing?

Me: Nothing lasts! What is the point of doing anything?

Phillip: Simply for the sake of doing it. Everything else is just waiting.

I have thought about this discussion for many years, and only now, on the threshold of falling apart myself, am I beginning to understand.

Once Upon A Time When I Was Myles

When online chat rooms were just beginning to be popular, we were advised by the various administrators to use caution when giving out personal information, and we were encouraged to use a nickname or create a 'nom de plume' as our 'screen name'. Being a writer, I was immediately drawn to this idea, and I created an alias: 'Myles'.

I discovered that I rather liked this fellow, Myles. I thoroughly enjoyed creating a fictitious personality and carefully filling in the details of his life, lest I be found out.

But there is an ethical border between fiction and lies. When someone believes your fabrication to be true and you do nothing to dispel the charade, you are lying.

I was surprised at how simple it was to weave a fictional story line and how strangely satisfying it was when someone believed me to be who I was pretending to be.

In my imaginary virtual world, there was a very real Renée who believed she had found a very real Myles. While she was busy unveiling the private details of her life, I was scripting an interactive fairytale, with a not-so-happily-ever-after ending.

When the fiction morphed into a lie, the conversation unfolded something like this:

Renée: So you're not really Myles?

Me: Well, I am kind of like Myles—Myles is someone I wish I were.

Renée: But your name is not really Myles, and you don't live in the wilds of Saskatchewan. And you don't really have a pet koala bear, do you? None of that is true.

Me: Your name isn't really 'Raven'. What's the difference?

Renée: Raven is my real nickname. I'm not pretending to be someone I am not; I am the person you think I am. You're a creep, a total poser, pretending to be someone you aren't.

Me: No. No, I'm not trying to *be* someone else. I am just creating a character and pretending to be him.

Renée: Yeah, that's what creeps do. I thought you were real, but all along, you were just goofing on me. I had genuine feelings for you.

Me: No, you had feelings for Myles, and I am sorry if you believed him to be real. I didn't think anyone on here took any of this seriously.

Renée: Yeah...well... Fuck You! How's that for real? You have broken my very real heart. I loved Myles, but now... Myles is dead to me!

Me: Yeah, Myles is dead. But Renée—

Renée is offline

I have since, for the most part, posed as myself. However, my adventures online taught me how much I enjoy creating characters, which led me to my first experiments in the writing of fiction.

Writing is a little like being naked. Regardless of how we adorn them or attempt to disguise them, words are sheer things that, when sewn together, create opaque paragraphs, exposing some delicate part of ourselves. Even when writing only to ourselves, as in a journal, we are standing naked in front of the mirroring page, analyzing parts of ourselves that we rarely examine. All the while, we are ever fearful that someone may one day read it, and yet, in our secret hearts, we hope someone will.

We want someone to know us—and yet we don't.

"Here, I'll show you this, and perhaps one day I will unclad that, but as for some things..."

So we text and sometimes message, but we rarely compose an entire expose' above or below a certain metaphorical hem, collar, or waistline.

As for blogging, well, blogging is a bit like flashing, isn't it? And while I suppose there is a bit of a voyeur and exhibitionist in all of us, we rarely go beyond partially clad. And perhaps that is as it should be. The imagination is always more intriguing than reality, Myles will attest to that. And maybe, just maybe, Raven, aka Renée, would as well.

Confessions of a Non-Joiner

I vaguely recall H. L. Mencken saying something like, "There is a pleasure those under the age of forty could never comprehend, called simply, 'Not going.'"

Through the years, I have received many invitations to all sorts of parties, and while I have always appreciated being invited, I doubt that my truancy reflected my gratitude. And so it is that these days, judging by the scarcity of requests for my presence, people are either having fewer parties or folks have stopped inviting me. I can't say I miss the parties I never attended, but I do miss being asked. There are, of course, exceptions.

When I was about 38 years old, I worked part-time in a call center with a group of teenagers. Being 20 years their senior, my social interaction with most of them was limited, but never mind; I was there to make money.

A young woman I'll call 'Fancy', who fancied herself Queen of the Fawning Tag Alongs, lorded over most of her ladies-in-waiting. She rarely spoke to me, and on the odd occasion when she actually acknowledged my presence, it was usually because I had somehow let slip a gaffe antithetical to her anal grasp on social norms.

She once said to me, "Wearing that white summer blazer the day after Labor Day is inconsiderate in the extreme."

I corrected her.

"No, my dear. My wearing a white summer blazer the day after Labor Day may be considered a minor social faux pas, but it is not inconsiderate. Vomiting on someone's birthday cake—*that* would be inconsiderate in the extreme."

You can imagine my surprise when Her Royal Highness approached me after work one day and asked,

"If I were to invite you to my birthday party, not that I am going to invite you, but should I invite you, would you accept?"

For a moment, the question scrambled all of my logical circuitry, and, after I had recovered my analytic equilibrium, I said,

"Well, if I were to accept, and I am not implying that I would accept, but before I would even consider accepting your possible invitation, I would need to know who else would be in attendance, because if my acceptance were based on my opinion of the host, I would have to, not so gratefully, decline."

To my surprise, the following day, she invited me to her party... and, in a momentary lapse of better judgment, I accepted!

I arrived about an hour late, and passing once through the room, I realized no one else from work had come. I did not know a single person in attendance, and I was, by a factor of two, older than the next oldest person in the room. After listening to people I didn't know talk about other people I didn't know and having a twelve-year-old explain how awesome his virtual reality goggles were—"Would I like to try them?" "No Thanks."—I let myself be coerced into a game of Harry

Potter Trivia. I have never (and I should have mentioned this at the time) read any of the Harry Potter books, watched any of the movies, or paid any attention to any discussion concerning Harry Potter. My 'teams' utter contempt for my complete ignorance of the subject was palpable.

One kid, flabbergasted by my inability to answer a single solitary question about the adventures of Master Potter or his cast of characters, growled, "What are you, a cave dweller?"

"Yes!" I answered, "I live in a cave, alright? And I really should be getting back before the fire goes out."

This seemed like a perfectly good exit line, and I had no more than thought the thought when Her Royal Highness handed me my coat and said, "I would like for you to leave my party." That, as it turns out, was a much better exit line.

"Okay," I said, "but before I go… where is that birthday cake of yours?"

***

One may conclude that I simply do not like people. But the truth is, I do. I like people. I actually enjoy small gatherings of people, but as soon as six or seven people huddle together, I can feel the 'chum' starting to permeate the atmosphere, and I gravitate toward an exit.

As a musician, I don't care for hootenannies; I shy away from jam sessions and steer clear of sing-a-longs. I am not a fan of group hugs. I am not a 'Kumbaya' kind of guy. I have no idea why I am this way. I had a relatively normal childhood. (I say "relatively" because no one has a *normal* childhood.)

I can remember being quite excited about *becoming* a cub scout. But once I actually *became* a cub scout, I could almost hear the air coming out of the tires. I looked around one day at all of us sitting in a circle, wearing a drab blue uniform and that squat, ill-fitting dopey cap with the yellow lines clawing at our heads, and I thought to myself, *'What the fuck am I doing here? Why am I sitting here, attempting to blend in with these goofy kids? Other than age, I have nothing in common with any of them.'*

After having suffered through an interminable evening in the woods with 'the troop', I decided I could no longer justify my participation in this 'pack' any longer, and to the best of my recollection, I do not believe I have had any social contact with any of them up to, and including, today. Not that they weren't nice people; they were. It is 'the group' with which I cannot abide. I am a social quitter— that's what I am.

To conclude, I should say, Dear Reader, I think it is best for all concerned if you and your friends would simply refrain from asking me to join in any of your reindeer games. I promise, I won't be offended, and to that end, neither will you.

11/4/2008

It has been a long, drawn-out loss of faith. But today, for the first time in forty years, I find myself wanting to believe again. It is such a fragile desire, but the fact that it has survived this long drought is either a testament to the power of hope or proof of the eternal naïveté of Homo sapiens.

I have been a political atheist since the morning of June 5th, 1968, when I awoke to the sound of my younger brother's voice.

"They shot his brother," was all he said—or needed to say. I knew immediately who had been shot. As far as who *they* were, it no longer mattered—*they* had won. The eclipse that began on November 22nd, 1963, was now total. If this sounds overly dramatic or poetic, it is not. Not to me.

In 1968, at the age of nineteen, I had just drawn my breath to give voice to my political self, even if the exact words failed me, even if the concepts of liberty, justice, and freedom were more of the heart than of the mind, I still wanted my voice to be heard. However, on the morning of June 6th, 1968, I held my breath, and I have held that breath and all the hope it contains for forty years, until tonight. Tonight, I exhaled.

Whatever words were taking shape in the mind and heart of that nineteen-year-old boy forty years ago are long lost to the vocabulary of another time. The words he has learned to use in the interim are far too cynical to be part of the dialog outlining the possibilities that now, at long last, lay before us. That narrative waits behind the lips of another generation, whose time has come. I envy their sense of hope. But I will say this: if hope is all you have, that is not enough.

Poetic PostScript: Tuesday, November 8th, 2016
Hope is just a town in Mississippi.
Faith is just a girl I used to know.
Charity covers up a multitude of crimes,
And beauty's just another fashion show.

Musings

Ah, Decadence

Ah, decadence! To go so far out on the thin of things that there is no longer a place called "From where you came."

We sometimes harbor the desire to crush the fresh and fragile, just as the fresh and fragile has been crushed in us. And sometimes, we wish to repair it, only to crush it again because we choose not to repair ourselves.

Decadence is not merely being out of rhythm with the marching band; it is dancing deliberately out of step, counter to the savagery of the unison.

Decadence is not depravity, any more than passion is indulgence, although we may, at times, indulge in our passion and, in doing so, descend into depravity. But fear not, the stepping out of bounds; fear more, the being bound.

Answers To... What Was The Question?

It has occurred to me lately that we have been a little too obsessed with answers. Answers are, of course, important, and most of the time, receiving an answer to a question we have asked is a good thing—usually—but not always.

Traditionally, the answer follows the question. But recently, it seems we have been bombarded with answers that have preceded the questions. I am being told the answers without having the benefit of knowing the questions asked. And because I have never had the opportunity to examine the inherent unasked question behind the pre-processed, pre-digested, pre-packaged answer, I could easily assume the answer I am being offered is correct. I have no choice, because, again, I do not know what the question is. I'm not even sure the people offering answers know the question or understand the issue. If that is true, many people are running around with answers to everything and solutions to nothing.

Considering these polarizing times, perhaps we shouldn't be too hasty in grasping for answers. It might be wiser if we were to spend more time formulating the right questions.

Properly framing the question enables us to investigate, clarify, and finally understand the problem. Understanding the problem is the compass pointing to the answer. The right answer to the wrong question is of no benefit. Only when we ask the correct questions can we profit from the right answer.

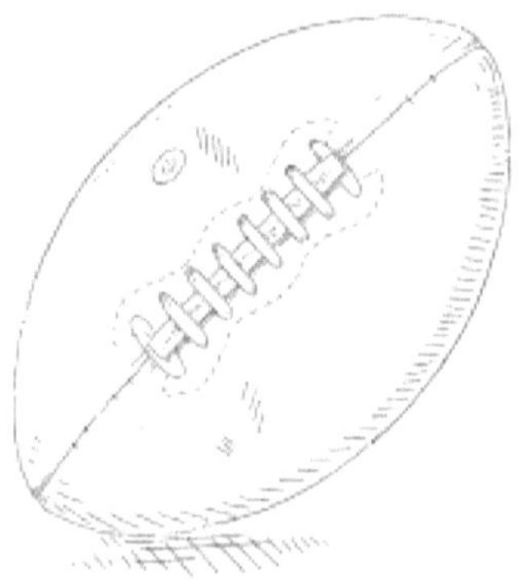

A Football Mystery

Okay, confession first: I am not your typical football fan. I don't enjoy the camaraderie of other football fans. As a matter of fact, I don't like to watch football in the presence of other people. I am a solitary spectator.

I don't care for any other sport: baseball bores me, basketball makes me nervous, soccer exhausts me, and hockey—well hockey is sort of soccer on ice, except I never know the location of the ball, I mean, puck.

I can't even tell you why I like football. But what *really* befuddles me is this: Why am I a Philadelphia Eagles fan? The favorite team of most people usually has something to do with proximity. I don't live anywhere near Philadelphia. Some folks pick teams according to the players. Since the advent of free agency, I can't name more than a few players on the Eagles in any given season. I've often wondered about the strength of a fan's allegiance if, say, in some unprecedented trade, Team A swapped all its players for Team B's. It takes a real sports heretic to even ponder such a ridiculous situation. Then there are those fans that love teams because of their winning tradition—everybody loves a winner—well, not everybody.

Here is a list of potential clues as to why I like the Eagles, followed by mysterious evidence to the contrary.

Clue #1: I started liking the Philadelphia Eagles around the age of 12, in 1960. This is the year they won the championship.

Mystery #1: Why would I have cared? The Cleveland Browns were a dynasty when I was growing up, winning the championship seven of the previous ten years. And Cleveland was only 100 miles north of my Ohio hometown. Chicago, Pittsburgh, Detroit, and even Baltimore had teams closer to me than the city of Philadelphia.

Clue #2: There was a player for the Eagles named Billy Ray Barnes. My name is Barnes.

Mystery #2: Jimmy Brown of the Cleveland Browns was my idol, and Elbie Nichol of the Pittsburgh Steelers lived down the street from me, and his boy Joe was one of my best friends. Plus, there was a guy named Erich Barnes who played for the Chicago Bears the same year the Eagles won the championship.

Clue #3: My junior high football team, on which I served as manager, wore the same color green jersey as the Philadelphia Eagles.

Mystery #3: I hate the color green.

The point is, for every reason I can conjure up to explain my allegiance to the Philadelphia Eagles, I can also produce a reason why I think it is a mystery.

This rarely bothers me, but every once in a while someone will ask,

"Oh, are you from Philadelphia?"

"No," I reply.

"Do you know someone on the team?" they ask.

"No," I reply.

"Then why do you like the Philadelphia Eagles?" they respond, more annoyed than curious.

"P-f-f-f-t, who knows?" I am forced to reply.

This usually results in the termination of the conversation. They cannot conceive of someone liking a team and yet not knowing why. They know why they like "their" team. "Their" team is the home team. For them, it comes down to turf.

But so what? It's not as if everyone on the team is from the immediate vicinity. There are teams that don't have a single player from anywhere near the state in which the team is located. I have a friend who has a brother who plays for the Miami Dolphins. Does this have any effect on his or her allegiance? Hell, No! He *hates* the Miami Dolphins.

Logically, I can't think of a single reason why I would be a sports fan, much less a fan of a particular team. However, my love of the Philadelphia Eagles, for no apparent reason, does not diminish my joy when they win or despair when they lose. I must find some sort of comfort in experiencing joy and despair over something that has no real relevance or consequence in my life. That is probably true of most fans. Go Eagles!

Richard Nixon: A Eulogy - 4/22/1994

A friend asked, "So, you were around during the Nixon era. What are your thoughts on his passing?"

This is a very complicated question, one that begs for a bottle of wine, someone's undivided attention, and plenty of time to reflect on the situation before simply reciting past platitudes-a-plenty.

My thoughts aside, my friend stood impatiently waiting for my answer, as if he had asked for the time of day.

So, I said, "It's like losing a rotten tooth. On the one hand, the pain is gone, but then again, so is the tooth."

He cocked his head, waiting for more....

"Look," I said, "Richard Nixon was the source of a great deal of pain and suffering for a staggering number of human beings. He made a mockery of the office of the President of the United States. His actions resulted in millions of otherwise optimistic human beings becoming disillusioned and paranoid about government for generations to come.

"I will not mourn Richard Milhous Nixon's passing; he was dead to me twenty years ago. But his death is a reminder of our complicity in the damage done because we elected him. We get the government we deserve."

When they write the history of the Nixon epoch, it may speak of a healthy, shining tooth that cut through foreign affairs with a sharp incisor's cut; ripped at complex geo-political issues with the separating precision of a well-honed bicuspid; chewed, with the patience of a mature molar, the historical prerogatives and consequences of various long-term political maneuvers—and that history needs to be told.

But let it also mention the aching, decayed, useless waste of precious resources and opportunity, rotten through to the root and now forever lost.

J. R. BARNES

Confession of a Ridiculous Man

So, it has come to this; I am empty. This lifelong quest for self-fulfill-ment has come to its absurdist conclusion. I have always been an empty vessel trying to fill itself with the self.

I have become so adept at the ability to satisfy myself that it has become an obsession. I am so saturated with the easily obtained plea-sure of 'gluttony of the self' that I have lost the ability to yearn. I am no longer qualified to cradle that desire that is insatiate; I have made a burnt offering of my passions so that I may satisfy my immediate lust.

What has become of my reaching arms, my calling voice, my simple awe of the horizon? Why can't I hear the distant voices that used to guide me? What has happened to my poetry? Where is the unwritten song that used to sting my heart and tease my creativity?

I am locked inside a mirror image of myself. I am no longer sure who is staring at whom. I sit atop a junk heap of *things*—possessions possessing me. I have confused purpose with pleasure and amused my-self unto oblivion.

IN OTHER WORDS

I have, at long last, consumed myself, and now, I am basking in my own waste, waiting... waiting to be flushed.

Got A Sec?

Just about everyone I talk to these days feels that time is going by much faster than it used to. It turns out there is some merit to this. As the result of a couple of earth quakes, one in Chile and the other in Sumatra, it seems the orbit of the earth has been altered enough to shorten the length of a day by about 8 microseconds. But this almost quantum spec of time cannot, in and of itself, account for millions of people saying, "I can't believe it's almost Christmas already!!!" No, something else is up; even if I take into account the fact that as we get older, our experiences tend to become less novel and time sort of compresses as one day blends into the next to form a big flabby glob of time called, "your life."

Which brings up another oddity of time. When you are experiencing something for the first time, time seems to fly, but the amalgam of these experiences in retrospect seems to make for a long and varied stretch of time. Childhood is an example of this. The span of time between the ages of 5 and 12 seems a hell-uv-a lot longer than the brief sojourn that is 35 to 42. And the bored moments that drag on while watching a series of insipid commercials while waiting for the return of the dopey sit-com you are marginally enjoying add up to the grand sum of... I'm 72! What the fuck happened to my life? The immediate effect is inversely proportional to the cumulative. But even if I take all of this into account, there is still *no way* that Christmas is only 21 days from now.

Here is what I think is happening. Everything has been quantized. Everything has been reduced in size, flattened, made more idiot-proof, child-proof, proof-proofed, dumbed down, pre-washed, pre-shrunk, pre-digested, iconized, marginalized, and abbreviated (we have an abbreviation for July...you gotta be in some kind of damn hurry!), so much so that it has literally changed the way we think. Our attention span has been significantly reduced to about 6 seconds, according to.... I forget where I was going with that. Our thoughts are shorter, our desires less complex, our relationships reduced to Facebook pages, and our communications truncated to texts. Nothing needs to last very long in a no deposit-no return, instant oatmeal world, and we like it that way. We don't want things to last because then they get old, and, damn it all, the *last* thing we want to be reminded of is that things age. We don't want to wait because then, without anything to entertain us, we get bored. It has to be NOW, and it has to be NEW, MODERN, IM-PROVED, and it has to go FASTER, FASTER, FASTER—we must go FASTER—and so it is; everything is going faster, even time itself. Because you don't see life as it is, you see life as you are. Thanks for your time...gotta run...

How She Hears Jingle Bells

I recently attended a recital of original music performed by a friend of mine; we'll call her Megan. Megan had recently received her Masters Degree in Composition from the North Texas College of Music and was the recipient of numerous awards, including a Grammy for a song recorded by a well-known jazz pianist.

At the post-concert reception, she informed me that a casual friend of ours had just invited her to a Christmas party, and she asked me if I was going. I told her probably not, and that, based on my experience of having attended the year before, I felt it only fair to warn her they would almost certainly ask her to play Christmas carols and various sundry tunes from the pop charts. She informed me she had no intention of playing the piano at the party, and so I reiterated my warning in stronger terms.

"You have no idea the pressure these people will bring to bear when they want to engage in a Christmas sing-along."

She smiled politely and brushed my warning aside.

At the party, several of the guests inquired about her piano playing and asked if maybe she would perform for them, to which she politely demurred, 'We'll see...

It was only a little while later that the well-quenched guests' simple request turned into group pleading. She tried to explain that she wasn't an entertainer per se, but a composer. So, naturally, they insisted she play one of her compositions.

She succumbed.

She was but a few measures into her composition when, judging by the furled brows and gaping jaws of the once-merry guests, the gaiety had all but evaporated from the room. Not a single person had the slightest grasp of what it was they were hearing, and so she cut short the performance; receiving a smattering of, why call it polite, applause?

"How about Jingle Bells?" someone called out.

My friend didn't respond immediately, taking her time to consider a polite refusal to the request.

"Oh, yes," someone applauded. "Do you know Jingle Bells?"

"I am familiar with the tune," she replied.

The host leaned in, and just above a whisper, she said to my friend, "I have the sheet music in the piano bench, if you need it."

Megan turned a quaint smile toward the host and began playing the simple little melody, one note at a time. She had thought of stopping after completing the first run through, but the crowd having chimed in with lyrics, she played the theme through again, this time with full chords, bass accompaniment, and grace notes. On the third go 'round, she began to explore the harmonic possibilities of the tune, altering the bass notes and modulating to parallel minor keys while changing both time signature and tempo. The vocal accompaniment quickly disintegrated, and people looked at one another as if she were telling a joke in a foreign language. She continued playing, although most of the revelers had either left the room or were otherwise engaged in conversation. When she returned to the simple little tune and played it out, a hush came over the remaining few gathered 'round.

She broke the silence, saying, "That is how I hear Jingle Bells. I'm sorry if you lost your hold on the melody."

When I saw her the following day, she told me of the experience and said, "I should have heeded your warning."

"No," I said. "I am glad you went. It is important for us as musicians to experience first-hand the dismissive indifference most people have as to the true nature of what it is we do and why we do it. They simply want to be entertained, and so they think of us as entertainers whose sole purpose is to serve up the familiar in as predictable a fashion as we know how—you know, music as a commodity. We can't expect them to understand, so sometimes we have to show them."

"Perhaps,' she said. "But I think I may have insulted them."

"Perhaps," I said. "But you are an artist, and an artist must explore. When someone asks you, as an artist, to perform, you need to seize that opportunity to take them on an adventurous journey into your imagination that they may experience your unique expressive qualities and interpretive abilities. Granted, they may not be aware of the scope and depth of their request, but you must respond as an artist.

She smiled cordially, as she so often does, giving no hint of whether she approved of my sentiments. I suppose every musician must find their own balance between their obligation to the audience and their fidelity to the music. I know that I still struggle with this.

If Only We Would All Believe

So, we were all called together and told, "If we all believe in this idea and work together, we can't help but succeed."

This was nothing new. I had heard this a thousand times before. Not the "idea," the bit about, "if we all believe."

It seems to me there is something terribly upside-down about this logic. To the casual observer, a good idea is distinguished from, say, "just an idea," by the benefits it bestows on the believers *and* the non-believers. A good idea does not necessarily require that you believe in it in order to benefit from it.

The light bulb requires no such universal faith. We benefit by virtue of it being a good idea. It may be true that someone has to believe in it, but this proposition that we *all* have to believe in *anything* appears rather uneconomical to me. I have noticed that sometimes, the more support an idea requires, the more horrendous the concept.

Just about any idea brought to fruition is going to bring some sort of benefit, real or imagined, to the believer.

I am very careful where I place my faith. There is something contemptuous about the "have faith first" approach that religious charlatans have banked on for millennia. Belief is powerful. So it is important that I carefully examine and reexamine what I believe. That is perhaps why I have a cerebral cortex, so that I may consider every available option before believing in any of them.

Beware of those who would save you from yourself. Eugene V. Debs once said, "I would not lead you into the promised land if I could, because if I led you in, someone else would lead you out."

Put another way, I would rather stay skeptically in place than go blindly, with a child's believing heart, toward someone else's vision of paradise.

But Socrates said it best. "The unquestioned life is not worth living." He may as well have added, and the unquestioned idea is not worth believing.

Lou Delivers Chester's Eulogy

So, my friend Lou is at this funeral for ol' Chester, and Chester's wife asks Lou if he'll say a few words. And Lou, he's stumblin' all over himself—at a loss for words, as they say.

So, all he's got is, "S'long old friend. Glad I got to know ya."

And his friends are gawkin' at Lou with a troublesome sneer, as if ta say, 'That's all you got ta say?'

So Lou, he turns to 'em and he says, "What else is there to say? I mean, the man's gone. He ain't here. Y'all are lookin' at the body of the car—the engine's long gone."

Billy Rae, he says, "WHAT? You're lookin' at your friend a-layin' there about ta be buried, and you're sayin', 'It's like when I lost my ol' Chevrolet?'"

And Lou says, "No, that ain't what I'm sayin'; that ain't what I'm sayin' a-tall. What I'm sayin' is, the man I knowd, the man I loved, the man I called my buddy—that man is solid gone. He ain't here. This body lyin' here is like the body of my old Chevy, when, one day, I was late for work 'cause she wouldn't start. And I called old Chester, and I said, 'Chester, my ol' Chevy won't start.'

"And Chester, he came over, raised the hood, and he said, 'Ain't no motor in this car.' And I said, 'What the hell are you talking 'bout? I drove this car to work just yesterday.' And Chester blinked a couple of times, shook his head, and says, 'Not this car as she sits here, you didn't. This'n ain't goin' nowhere.'"

Billy, he's starin' at Lou like he's got a third eyeball, and Lou says to him, "Now, as to where that motor went, I do not know. And so it is; our friend's body a-layin' here, is like a car that ain't goin' nowhere. It's a beautiful piece of work, but here it lays—nothin' but a mem'ry. I do not know where Chester's motor went; it ain't for to say, no how. I know that the motor that powered this man was a well-tuned machine that hummed forth, hittin' on all eight, always on a mission. And I know that I enjoyed drivin' alongside him on many an adventure. It weren't a matter of where we was goin', so much as a matter of who we were going there with. And yeah, too bad he's gone and all, but he woulda wanted us to move on. And so, S'long, old friend. I'm glad I knew ya."

Chester's wife, she came up to Lou, gave him a big hug, and said, "Lou, that was beautiful."

Misery

It's the same thing every day. I wake up and ask myself, "At long last, what is the point?" I have yet to unravel the conundrum, so I make my peace with the absurdities and go forth into the world, doing my best not to infect anyone with my existential angst. Let the 'I just want to be happy' hoard high-step through the discord, whistling "What A Wonderful World" as the muck rises up around their fashionable footwear. I wish them well; anyone who believes in the pursuit of happiness deserves exactly what is coming to them.

As for me, I believe happiness is demonstrably overrated. But I try not to depress anyone because most people do not deserve to be miserable. Nine-tenths of them wouldn't know misery if it showed up at their door, formally introduced. And even if you could convince them that they are, in fact, miserable, they are so hell bent on being happy, they wouldn't know how to properly wallow in it. They simply do not give misery the same respect as their ancestors—*they* were a hearty lot!

By the age of ten, most of our forbearers had borne more misery than the average woe-begotten soul at present bears in a lifetime. Why, they practically reveled in their own misery, and given the odd Sunday away from the drudgery of their fruitless labors, they all congregated in little houses of worship to listen to the stories of their biblical ancestors' miseries. Then, thanking their creator in a hail of hosannas, they traipsed off to splash around in their own squalor until the glorious day when they could finally cry out, "Dead at last, dead at last, thank God almighty, we are dead at last!"

I think what I like most about misery is that it is the one thing that I can lay claim to without much of an argument from my fellow beings. It is all mine, either of my own doing or of the sort referred to as "just my luck!" Rarely, if ever, is anyone envious of it, and to my recollection, not a breathing soul has ever connived to fetch it from me.

Happiness is such an elusive and fickle thing. Misery is a stalwart companion. It greets us in the morning, accompanies us throughout our dismal day, and tucks us into our debtor's bed at night. Oh, the constant reminder that life is a series of disappointments, save for those precious moments when we are too weary to care.

It is a shame that so many people walk through life wearing blinders and knee-high boots while seeking analgesic after analgesic in a pact with the devil to achieve comfort in this life. There are times when I want to cry out to them, "Off with your boots and blinders. Come slosh in the muck and free yourself from the tyranny of Abraham's bosom."

But I am reminded that a misery shared is but half the misery, so I selfishly greet them with a smile and a sincerely expressed, "Have a nice day."

My Facebook Friends And Me

Here I am on Facebook again, scrolling through pictures of someone's dinner, reels and short videos, clever quips on a colored background, tons-o'-ads, an occasional personal post, and my favorite thing, an actual message.

However, lately, I have come to wonder whether Facebook is friend-friendly. It seems friendly enough at first glance. After all, according to Facebook, I have over a thousand friends.

Of course, no one really has a thousand friends; if you are fortunate enough to have five truehearted friends, you are fortunate enough. Most of my Facebook 'friends' are colleagues, sidekicks, longtime acquaintances, and social chums. There are a few I probably *should* remember, and some of them, I am fairly certain, are total strangers. If I were to somehow find myself alone with this one fellow that calls himself "Gumball," I would be at a complete loss for the words with which to begin a conversation.

Still, no harm done. Maintaining a virtual friendship is the lightest of chores. What concerns me is the maintenance of an actual friendship, one that has developed and been nurtured throughout the years.

Friendship requires a certain amount of work. It is sometimes difficult and, frankly, inconvenient to stay in touch and interact in a meaningful way with our friends. I personally have a terrible track record in this regard. So naturally, I thought Facebook was designed for people like me. I could now stay self-absorbed and maintain friends with a minimal amount of effort. Well, it just doesn't work that way.

I sometimes wonder if Facebook has, at times, proved to be an actual detriment to the intricate fabric of friendship. Oh sure, we "Like" each other's comments; we "Share" each other's memes; we reply to comments about shared memories; we comment on photos of events we wish we had attended; and sometimes we actually message one another. But what if there was no Facebook? Then, perhaps, I would write, call, visit, or otherwise actually connect with my friends... perhaps...

Still, I worry. Are the actual friends I have loved and cared about 'lo these many years, these friends who are now more important than ever—are these precious few companions gradually becoming virtual friends that I simply wave to, now and then, as I virtually cruise by on my way to...

NO

I recently read an article stating that children learn to say no at a very early age, and having learned the power of the word, it becomes their mantra, much to their parents' chagrin. The article explained that this is a normal sign of childhood development; it is a child asserting their independence.

I must have gone through this developmental stage, although around the age of seven, I remember my mother saying, "What is the matter with you? Don't you know how to say no?" Evidently, very early on, I had a problem with this simplest of monosyllabic sounds.

If so, it could be because I prefer, and have a particular fondness for, the word 'yes'. I love everything about 'yes'. 'Yes' has led me to the most wonderful experiences of my life. To be fair, it has taken me deep into the badlands as well. However, having survived those trips, I don't regret having made them, even though, in retrospect, I sometimes wonder, 'What the hell was I thinking?' In other words, I probably should have said, 'no'.

When I was forty years old, my employer called me into her office and said, "While I commend you on your dedication to customer satisfaction, you have got to learn how to say no!"

Forty years old!

I decided the solution to this problem was to have a batch of business cards printed up with just the word NO placed right in the middle, and when someone asked me to do something I didn't want to do, I could say, "I'll get back with you" and send him or her my card.

I ordered one thousand satin black business cards with the word no printed in capital letters in a gold Cambria Bold font. The day I received them, I carried them into my supervisor's office, opened the box, pulled out a card, and handed it to her. She furrowed her brow and asked, "What the hell is this?" She turned the card toward me, and there, right in the middle of the satin black card, in gold Bold Cambria capital letters, was the word ON.

I said, "No, you...you've got it upside—" and I stopped short of explaining. I realized that regardless of how I attempt to avoid it, I live in the world of yes. Oh, and no, I will not apologize for it any longer.

Oh, To Be 21 Again?

I'm an old man. I like being an old man. If it were possible for me to be 21 again I am not certain I would take advantage of the opportunity.

Do I have to be 21 again at the loss of what I know now, or do I get to retain an old man's perspective? I really wouldn't trade what I have learned just so I can learn it all again—that seems like a goofy thing to do. And if I were to retain all that I have learned over all these years, wouldn't my peers view me as an insufferable bore? It also occurs to me that being an old man in the body of a 21-year-old, would take all the fun out of being 21; the novelty of uncertainty has its own rewards, although at the time it doesn't seem that way; you have to live a few years to understand that.

You have to live a few years to understand so many things, such as the fact that no matter how much you know, you really don't know much about anything. When you understand that, the world is filled with wonder again.

So, no. I like being an old man. I don't want to be a young man in love again any more than I want a new bicycle. It has taken me a long time to get here, and it has been one hell of a ride. I don't believe in reincarnation, but I wish it were so. I'd love to come back as me again—it's been a gas.

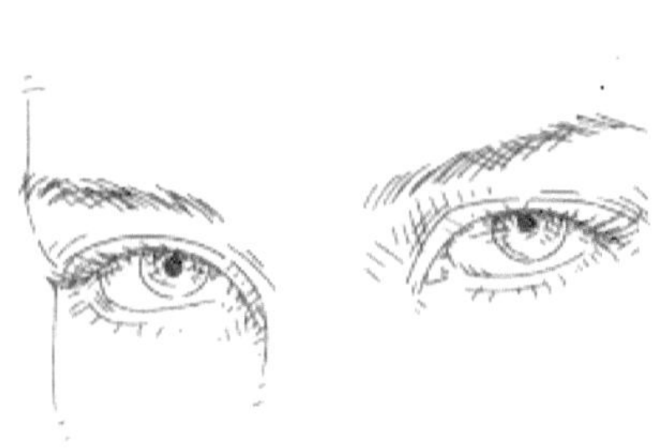

Seduction

Women seduce men. Let me say at the outset that I am not using the word seduce in the negative sense; substitute the word entice if you wish. The seduction I am speaking of is the most natural of things—among women; men only think they seduce women. I am eternally grateful for the seductive wiles of women; my intent here is simply to set the record straight.

Sometimes women prefer to believe they were seduced because it relieves them of a certain responsibility. But in truth, the illusion of her surrender is something men cannot resist, and whether she knows it or not, she is the one in control.

Men like to *think* they seduce women because it boosts their under-developed ego and perpetuates their bogus belief in male superiority, i.e., women simply cannot resist us—what a wonderful world. Howev-er, the fan dance performed by the male of almost every species is noth-ing more than an attempt to prove himself worthy of her seduction.

All men, so oriented, pursue women, and we do so with sex in mind. If we try not to let it drip from our words, if we attempt to hide the fact that we are negotiating our way into their nether regions, it is merely out of some sense of décor. We feel it is gauche to blurt out our hidden desires. We fear most women would find it repulsive, or worse, humorous. And rightly so; after all, we are taking away their prerogative. A man could no more seduce a woman than a horse could ride a man. We will do what we can and go to any lengths to get them to seduce us, believing all the while that testosterone trumps estrogen—what a farce!

The answer to the age-old question "What do women want?" is obvious—they want you to pay attention. So, you can stop trying to 'pick up' women. They already know if they are interested in you... all you need to do is pay attention.

Taking My Time

Many folks put off chores, duties, and various tasks of an unpleasant nature. This is a quite common reaction that may be viewed by some as irksome, but it does not rise to the level of procrastination.

We, the card-carrying procrastinators, have perfected the art of hanging fire. We linger on the fringe, regardless of reward. We dally, dawdle, delay, and loiter. We like to take our time. We love our time. We bask in our time. We will lollygag our way through the day, rarely glancing at the second hand, or at clocks at all, for that matter. Our lives are but a series of moments. And given the time, we will connect those moments, as only a procrastinator can, into a meaningful whole. We do not force things to happen before their time. We like to make love to the world, and the more foreplay, the better! We do *not* multitask, and we have an inherent distrust of those who believe in such balderdash. Do one thing at a time, do it well, take your time, and, above all, put it off.

Have you asked yourself, what is the point of all this hurrying? I would like to know who is benefiting from my turning my life into a series of eight-hour dashes. Who are these people that measure my endeavors in terms of efficiency—efficiency for whom? And after these deadlines have come and gone, and I lay spent, too tired to yawn, where are all the fucking cheerleaders then?

No, no, no, and no again. If you want me to do something and I surrender to your wishes, by all means, give me a deadline, because if you don't, something else will catch my fancy, and well, I'm bound to follow my fancy. But after we agree on the deadline, don't tell me when to start, don't ask for progress reports, and don't expect me to hand it in prematurely. Because right up to the deadline, I am going to be hitting the snooze alarm and taking another nine minutes of my life to do with them exactly as I please. If I have agreed to deliver, I will deliver. It will be loosely wrapped and carelessly twined, but the contents will be of a quality worthy of my word. I've never trusted or cared that much about packaging. I leave that for those who love to tie bows and finish the task early enough to do so.

The Moment

All we have as children is the here and now—the moment. We don't really own anything; we don't have a job; we literally have no control over the future; and tomorrow, as in the next day, is a long way off. Each day is a day unto itself.

By the time we are in our teens, hormones have crept up from our nether regions, and we become inordinately focused on the nether regions of other people. We have already learned that the road to bliss is the one lined with shopping centers, and that money is more important than intelligence, and that looks are more important than money. We are no longer kids, but we are not yet adults. And so we live in the in-between; each day is just one more day in another boring waiting room.

As we ooze into our 20s, our thoughts turn to family. Not the one that brought us here and sustained us thus far, but the one that we are about to start. We are now Major League Consumers. We are buying REALLY BIG THINGS, and trying to save for our future at the same time. Each day is spent reminiscing about our past, fretting about our present financial situation, and worrying about the future.

Our 30s find us buried in our work. The family that we were so eager to start and that was so important just a few years ago now takes a back seat to our job. Money begets more money. We are now more concerned about the future than the present, and each day is spent wondering when the weekend will get here or wondering where the hell it went.

By the time we are 40, we are starting to wonder what happened. Our kids are either gone or soon to be, and while we are looking forward to a little peace and quiet, it never dawns on us that we have *never* experienced peace and quiet, so why are we looking forward to something that would probably scare the Holy Ghost out of us? We are not yet ready for peace and quiet. As each day melds seamlessly into the next, what we actually yearn for are the fresh passions of our youth. We are not yet old, but we are no longer young. We are of two hearts—one holding on, the other letting go.

Our 50s are spent examining our own bodies. Things are starting to mutate and malfunction. We can't help but notice that while we feel like we are 25, it has been longer than 25 years ago since we were 25. To the vast majority of people in a youth-oriented culture, we are invisible. Each day reminds us that, whatever that thing was that we were waiting on, it has already gone.

Our 60's are spent in a time warp. The future isn't what it used to be. There just isn't a whole lot of that thing called 'the future' left. Our short-term plans are now our long-term plans. The past, which makes up the majority of our lives, seems ludicrously compact. Each day is more past than present, and we have come to understand destiny as something that has already happened.

Should we make it to our 70s, we have accumulated many things, but fewer are the ones that matter. We don't have a job, and there is very little, if any, future to have any control over. There is precious little left but the moment, which we finally realize is what we should have been living in all along, but of course, even now, it isn't too late. Cherish the moment you're in, regardless of your age.

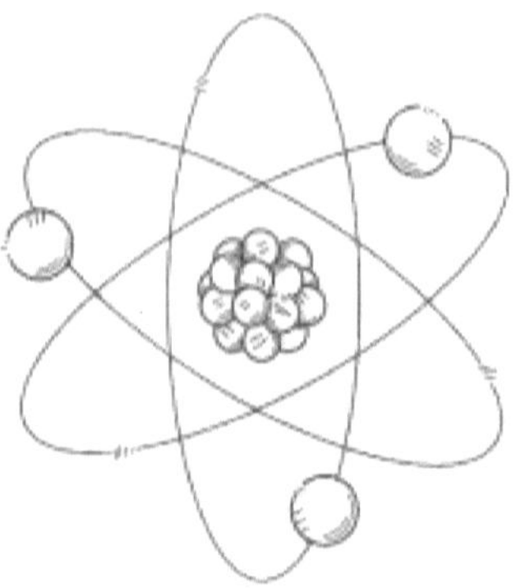

The Tiniest Thing

This is the story of the tiniest thing that we, as humans, know about. So tiny is this object that it can pass, unaffected, through anything. It is smaller than the smallest space between any two things, even things that are so small they boggle our huge thoughts—things like electrons and protons and neutrons and -ons not yet discovered.

So small is our central character that we can't actually measure it in any known traditional way. It is a point-like particle far too small to be seen with even the most powerful microscope. It is 1000 times smaller than a proton, which is 100,000 times smaller than an atom. That is to say, incomprehensibly small.

Our tiniest thing may only exist for 5×10 to the minus 25th power of a second. This time span is theoretical because it is 100,000 times smaller than the shortest span of time we are capable of measuring. But of course, according to its way of thinking, it has lived a full and quite normal lifetime.

The name of our character is Quark. And now, on with our story.

IN OTHER WORDS

The Tiniest Thing

Once upon a time, there was a quark.

The End

These Gray and Thinning Days

I sometimes forget how old I am. While this can be a liberating respite, every sinew of my aging body reminds me that my full-throttle, devil on steroids, get-the-hell-outta-my-way days are over. I maintained that rapacious rampage for much longer than I should have, resulting in my not so much slowing down as coming to an abrupt halt around the age of fifty-two.

After convalescing in neutral for a while, I came to realize I had not been in Drive for quite some time and that whatever speed I was currently cruising at was because I was going downhill.

A friend, who is a few years my senior, told me I needed to pay closer attention to my body. He reminded me that, while I may deny it, I am on the wane. "Biologically speaking," he said, "you are in reverse, and, well, you know what it is like to drive in reverse."

I do indeed.

To all of us who have been fortunate enough to 'come of age' and find ourselves in reverse, biologically speaking, I believe it would serve us better to proceed with a little more caution than is sometimes comfortable, and wisdom would advise us to slow down and take careful aim. We may be in reverse, but we are still moving forward; we remain purposeful beings.

The vista is unfolding into an ever-receding horizon, just as it always has. Take heart; we are still the pilots at the wheel, and with a bold frame of mind and a little faith in distance, we are, each of us, quite capable of enjoying the ride. Good luck to you, and try to stay in your own lane.

'Tis Spring Again

Today is the first day of spring. I will at some point during the day burst out into song, not because it is the first day of spring, but because I burst out into song, at one point or another, every day.

Yesterday it was 'Bus Stop' by The Hollies. The day before, I was seized upon to belt out 'Chances Are', making no attempt what-so-ever to mimic the great Johnny Mathis—no one can, but never mind, it is a great song that lends itself to many voices.

This constant, somewhat dotty, spontaneous eruption of song was undoubtedly the result of my association with my sister Suanne and her friend, Trudy. The two of them would spark at the opportunity to turn any of life's more mundane moments into a scene from a Rodgers and Hammerstein musical, the unwitting audience notwithstanding. I always admired their bravado.

Who knows what song will emerge from my noggin' today, but I doubt it will have anything to do with the Spring Equinox, unless that song is George Gershwin's 'But Not For Me'.

IN OTHER WORDS

I understand the arrival of spring and all it brings to the hearts of those who have finally shed their winter clothes in favor of their sunnier things, but not for me—my life usually comes apart at the stitches every spring. I will not dwell on this; I am not saddened beyond a sigh, and I am quite accustomed to the routine.

I found this little ditty that I wrote many years ago. It sums it up in verse:

'Tis Spring Again
Although it's spring, I must confess,
Each April leaves my heart a mess,
And May has never been much help.
June's obsessed with herself,
And her friend July is one big lie,
With whiskey on her breath,
And the stale sweat of August,
Stains September's dress.
Ah-h, but I love October,
And I'm glad that summer's over,
As I await winter's long refrain,
Knowing full well, it is only a spell
'Till spring returns again.

To A Teacher

It is a bit like trying to explain music with words, relationships are. They each have their own unique tempo, rhythm, melodic structure, harmonies, dissonances, etc. I'm sure you have had the experience of hearing a song for the first time and somehow immediately knowing that this song was going to stay with you for a while. That is the essence of my first meeting with you. I simply knew that you were someone I was guided to. I don't pretend to understand anything about such forces but I do believe, as Robert Frost said, way leads on to way.

I do know there are melodies and rhythms and tempos that we are drawn to because they are who we are. I have learned that the song I am trying so hard to write is actually already written. I am merely the transcriber/performer. Our job is to sing as honestly as we can to anyone who will listen and the words will come.

Upon our first meeting, I was taken by your song. I heard it in your smile. Your smile is not a reflection, nor is it a mere expression. Your smile is who you are. It is an honest smile. It radiates from you. Your song is in your eyes. Through your eyes, the world perceives itself. They cast their own light enabling others to see as well. They are the eyes of a teacher, a teacher with vision. A teacher who understands that teaching is a form of touch. And whether it is obvious to you or not, we are touched by you—we are captured by your song.

I realize that I have only known you for a short period of time. I realize that you have dark passages and notes out of key and, (extending the metaphor), unfinished compositions. But, dear teacher, I am a musician, and I know a beautiful melody when I hear one.

What Really Killed Michael Jackson

"...extraordinary people live extraordinary lives."
This is a quote I came across concerning the eccentric lifestyle and the demise of Michael Jackson. Evidently, this is an attempt to explain to the rest of us "ordinary people" why Jackson, Presley, Hendrix, Morrison, and __________ (fill in the blank) died before their time. This, of course, is bullshit. They died of a systematic abuse of drugs that kills hundreds of people every single day, extraordinary or not.

The people mentioned above had extraordinary talents, to be sure, but they were not extraordinary human beings. They were normal people with normal frailties. They had the same insecurities, fears and, mixed bag of emotional slippery slop that all of us have. The tragedy is that they never really had to deal with it. They surrounded themselves with people who always said yes to them and showered them with praise. So, even on those rare occasions when someone dared to disagree or tell them the bad news, they could easily and conveniently ignore them.

If everyone agreed with you all the time, regardless of how whacked-out your logic appeared; if we all laughed at your jokes, regardless of whether we thought they were funny; waited on your every whim, never minding how destructive it was; and treated you as if you were special, you would come to believe that you were an extraordinary human being.

What killed Michael Jackson is the same thing that killed Elvis Presley. He came to believe that he was MICHAEL JACKSON... and no one dared tell him otherwise. What all of this means for the rest of us is this: The next time a friend tells you, "You are fucking up!" you might want to stop and give it some thought. You may even want to thank them. They may be trying to save your life.

While Watching The Leaves Of Summer Fall

When I was a child, I would be filled with mixed emotions as I watched the painted leaves of summer lilting their way to the ground, embroidering our yard with a multi-colored quilt, but of course, I knew I would eventually have to rake them up. This act, the raking of the leaves, made no sense to me—not that it mattered. I was a kid, and kids have to rake leaves.

My father insisted that the task be done every week, starting in September and ending when the last leaf or the first snow fell. He reasoned that by doing it every Saturday morning, the task wasn't as difficult, and the lawn always looked *nice*. I reasoned, Why not just wait until all the leaves have fallen and rake them all at once? His method did not always leave the lawn looking *nice*. It only looked *nice* on Saturdays, immediately after I raked it.

What was the problem with leaves lying on the ground? I have taken many walks in the woods. I don't recall ever having thought, 'You know, these woods are a mess! Someone ought to rake up all of these leaves so that the wilderness looks *nice*.'

I once asked my father, "What happens to the leaves on the ground in the woods?"

"They turn into next year's soil to nurture the trees and other plants," was his wise reply.

"Well..." and I just stood there waiting for him to realize what a nincompoop he had been all of his life for raking the leaves every Saturday in the fall, and he was even now passing that absurd, ecologically unsound tradition on to his sons, but alas, the circuit never closed.

My father would much rather bundle them up in big plastic bags and throw them "away," wherever that is. Probably some place that pours them back on the ground, lets them turn back into soil, re-bags them in plastic bags, and sells them to my father the following spring so that he can spread them once again throughout the yard.

I continued to rake leaves every Saturday in the autumn until my younger brother inherited the ridiculous task. Now that I have my own lawn, I do it my way; I leave them to turn into next year's soil. My neighbors seem a little annoyed, but it is something they are simply going to have to deal with. My younger brother makes his son rake the leaves every Saturday from September until November.

One beautiful Saturday afternoon in October, I tried to point out to him the finer points of my theory concerning his son's efforts out on the lawn. He wasn't very receptive to my logic. I don't know if this is because he is a father now, and that implies a kind of peculiar empirical logic, i.e., he had to rake leaves every Saturday in the fall; therefore, his boy has to rake leaves every Saturday in the fall. It doesn't really matter. Because all of those fathers and I have at least one thing in common—none of us have to rake the leaves every Saturday this fall.

Also by j. r. Barnes

Sailing Home
The Blue Rose
In Other Words